LEARNING MATH WITH

Calculators

ACTIVITIES FOR GRADES 3–8

LEARNING MATH WITH
Calculators
ACTIVITIES FOR GRADES 3–8

LEN SPARROW & PAUL SWAN

Math Solutions Publications
Sausalito, CA

Math Solutions Publications
A division of
Marilyn Burns Education Associates
150 Gate 5 Road, Suite 101
Sausalito, CA 94965
www.mathsolutions.com

Library of Congress Cataloging-in-Publication Data
Sparrow, Len.
     Learning math with calculators : activities for grades 3–8 / Len Sparrow, Paul Swan.
          p. cm.
     Includes bibliographical references.
     ISBN 0-941355-35-7 (alk. paper)
     1. Mathematics—Study and teaching (Elementary) 2. Mathematics—Study and teaching (Middle school) 3. Calculators. I. Swan, Paul. II. Title.
QA135.6 .S63 2001
372.7—dc21

                                                                            2001003873

Editor: Toby Gordon
Production: Melissa L. Inglis
Cover design: Catherine Hawkes/Cat and Mouse Design
Interior design: Joni Doherty Design
Composition: Tom Allen

Printed in the United States of America on acid-free paper
05 04 03 02   ML   2 3 4 5

A Message from Marilyn Burns

We at Marilyn Burns Education Associates believe that teaching mathematics well calls for continually reflecting on and improving one's instructional practice. Our Math Solutions Publications include a wide range of choices, from books in our new Teaching Arithmetic series—which address beginning number concepts, place value, addition, subtraction, multiplication, division, fractions, decimals, and percents—to resources that help link math with writing and literature; from books that help teachers more deeply understand the mathematics behind the math they teach to children's books that help students develop an appreciation for math while learning basic concepts.

Along with our large collection of teacher resource books, we have a more general collection of books, videotapes, and audiotapes that can help teachers and parents bridge the gap between home and school. All of our materials are available at education stores, from distributors, and through major teacher catalogs.

In addition, Math Solutions Inservice offers five-day courses and one-day workshops throughout the country. We also work in partnership with school districts to help implement and sustain long-term improvement in mathematics instruction in all classrooms.

To find a complete listing of our publications and workshops, please visit our Web site at *www.mathsolutions.com*. Or contact us by calling (800) 868-9092 or sending an e-mail to *info@mathsolutions.com*. We're eager for your feedback and interested in learning about your particular needs. We look forward to hearing from you.

A DIVISION OF MARILYN BURNS EDUCATION ASSOCIATES

▼ CONTENTS

▼ INTRODUCTION

Calculators and Controversy

Calculators are not new. They have been available to the general public for over twenty years. Many people use them every day; some carry a calculator with them wherever they go. Why, then, is their use so problematic with respect to elementary and middle school mathematics teaching?

Educators have advocated using calculators in mathematics teaching for a number of years. In the United States some of the earliest thinking on calculator use in the schools came from the National Council of Teachers of Mathematics (NCTM) in *An Agenda for Action: Recommendations for School Mathematics in the 1980s* (1980), where it was noted that "[m]athematics programs must take full advantage of the power of calculators and computers at all grade levels." Similar assertions were made in the United Kingdom (Cockcroft 1982) and Australia (Australian Association of Mathematics Teachers 1986).

Yet more than twenty years after the NCTM made its recommendation, calculators continue to have little impact on how mathematics is taught in elementary and middle schools, let alone on the content of that teaching. In fact, many people—parents, educators, and administrators alike—would like to ban calculator use in the classroom, citing fears that children will become reliant on them at the cost of developing proficiency in mathematics. And yet there is little research evidence that supports these fears. In fact, studies point in the opposite direction, by showing that sensible use of calculators in the elementary and middle school classroom leads to improved ability in mathematics.

Aims and Purpose of This Book

Our general aim is to support teachers in developing sensible ways to use calculators in the classroom and so help children mature as better and more confident mathematicians. Specifically, we attempt to:

- address issues raised by classroom teachers regarding calculator use
- provide clear links between calculator use and the elementary and middle school mathematics curriculum
- address questions raised by parents and others related to calculator use
- further an understanding of how calculators can engage children in thinking about mathematics and support conceptual understanding
- offer commentary on and examples of activities designed to incorporate sensible calculator use

Why Should We Use Calculators to Teach Math?

In general terms, we should use calculators in the teaching of math in order to:

- help children develop number sense
- help children develop mathematical ideas and understand connections, relationships, and patterns
- acquaint children with technology
- respond to national standards
- put into action the findings of educational research

Helping Children Develop Number Sense

Number sense is an important idea in mathematics teaching. It is underpinned by the fundamental idea that children (and adults) should and can make sense of numbers. This seems obvious, but for many people numbers do not make sense. Number sense implies that children should deal with numbers in confident and flexible ways. They should have a variety of strategies they can use to approach a problem, and they should be able to select the most appropriate strategy for its completion.

There are two general ways in which a calculator may help children to develop number sense—as a computational tool and as a teaching and learning aid.

The calculator as a computational tool. The calculator allows children to work with numbers in ways that they would not be able to do with pencil and paper. In this sense, the calculator allows children to work with messy, real-life data. The calculator here is used as a computational tool, purely for its ability to deal easily and quickly with large numbers and complex data.

Because the calculator enables students to work with such material quickly and accurately, they can focus on the mathematical concept underlying the computational task. An example of how the calculator plays this role is shown in Section 2, in the activity Finding Pi?

The calculator as a teaching and learning aid. The calculator can also help children to think about numbers in different ways. In this sense, the calculator is used as a teaching and learning aid, much as students might use manipulatives. Teachers who are just beginning to use calculators in their classrooms often feel most comfortable with this mode of use. Activities reflecting such use are often highly defined and less likely to provoke the criticism that children are relying on calculators rather than thinking for themselves. A typical example of a calculator being used as a teaching aid is the game Wipeout, in which children are instructed to enter into the calculator a four-digit number (e.g., 4761) and then remove one of the digits (e.g., 7) by subtraction. Removing the 7 requires subtraction by 700 and an understanding of numeric face and place value. A fuller description of this activity is offered in Section 2.

Helping Children Develop Mathematical Ideas and Understand Connections, Relationships, and Patterns

An important aim of mathematics teaching is to help children understand that mathematics concerns relationships and patterns. The calculator can be a useful tool in helping children to develop this insight. The activity Multiplying by 10 in Section 2 is an example of how calculators can support learning important mathematical concepts.

The idea underlying Multiplying by 10 is that whole numbers and decimals follow a consistent pattern when they are multiplied or divided by 10 and powers of 10. Having an understanding of this concept allows children to develop a mental facility for multiplying and dividing numbers by 10, 100, 1,000, and so on. In doing this activity, it is important that children discuss and reflect on how the pattern changes with respect to multiplication and division and from whole numbers to decimals. This observation should help children understand how to quickly multiply or divide by 10 and powers of 10 without having to resort to the quick, but in many cases incorrect, add-a-zero rule often employed with whole numbers but not applicable to decimals.

Acquainting Children with Technology

Although critics often cite the use of calculators in elementary and middle schools as one reason for low math aptitude among schoolchildren, according to research, calculator use in elementary and middle schools is limited. In fact, many eleven-year-old children in Britain were unable to cope with the requirements of a national test that demanded explicit use of calculators. They ignored the calculator options and resorted to standard pencil-and-paper methods for calculating. In the United States, one group of sixth graders reportedly rejected calculators in situations in which their use would be appropriate, because they were unable to understand the decimal display on the machine. Since their knowledge of division was limited to whole numbers and remainders, they were unable to interpret the decimal notation shown on the calculator. For many children (and adults), many of the keys on even the simplest of calculators (for example, the memory functions) are not used, because they never learned how to use them. Mathematics instruction that does not acknowledge the presence and power of calculators and that does not teach children how to use the calculator effectively and efficiently will continue to produce members of society who are "calculator ignorant."

Therefore, another reason for using the calculator in elementary and middle schools is to help children understand how and when its use is appropriate. It is the job of the teacher to help children become "calculator-aware." A calculator-aware child is able to make an informed choice about using, or not using, a calculator for a given computation. Effective teaching with calculators involves preventing children from becoming overreliant on these tools to the extent that they are used for even simple calculations.

Responding to National Standards

The Principles and Standards for School Mathematics (NCTM 2000) recently added to the points made earlier in *An Agenda for Action*; the "technology principle" of this document states that "[t]echnology is essential in teaching and learning mathematics; it influences the mathematics that is taught and enhances students' learning" (24).

In fact, curriculum documents in the United States, the United Kingdom, and Australia widely recommend that calculators be used to:

- support and extend students' mathematics-learning experiences
- develop mathematics proficiency within a technologically rich learning environment

◆ help children understand and use the features of a basic calculator, interpreting the display in the context of the problem and using the constant function, memory, and brackets to plan a calculation and evaluate expressions

Putting Research Findings into Action

Although research into calculator use at the elementary and middle school levels is limited, findings offer a positive view of such use. Major reports have come from the Calculators in Primary Mathematics (CPM) project in Australia, the Calculator Aware Number (CAN) and Calculator as a Cognitive Tool (CCT) projects in the United Kingdom, and two research metanalyses in the United States (Hembree and Dessart 1986; 1992).

Used correctly, the calculator can be a powerful agent for change in the classroom. Reports from the CAN and CPM projects indicate that children made many gains in mathematics as a result of the introduction of calculators, which changed the way mathematics was taught in the project schools. The use of calculators caused teachers to reexamine their methods, assumptions, and philosophy of mathematics teaching. This served to highlight the calculator's role in

◆ enabling both teachers and children to focus on the development of number sense
◆ fostering positive attitudes and persistence with respect to mathematics
◆ furthering children's strategies when faced with a calculation
◆ increasing students' ability to solve problems in their heads and with pencil and paper
◆ eliminating the need for strict conformity to fixed sets of procedures in solving equations

The calculator is one of the best tools for developing computational choice, if it is used to further children's thinking about numbers. Results from the CPM project (Groves and Stacey 1998) indicated that children "made more appropriate choices of calculating devices" and that "there was no evidence that children became reliant on calculators at the expense of their ability to use other methods of computation" (128). Hembree and Dessart (1986; 1992) reported similar findings in the research studies they looked at in the United States, and noted that children's mathematical aptitude improved with the introduction of calculators into the classroom.

Using This Book

We do not intend for this book to be read from beginning to end. A suggested method of use is to look through the questions in Section 1, read those that are of particular interest to you or most relevant to your classroom practice, and try out with your students the activities presented in Section 2. The math goal of each activity is identified based on the conceptual understanding or ability the activity is intended to support. The activities are particularly aimed at children in grades three through eight. Each activity is marked with a grade range of three to five or six to eight, but this is only a suggestion. You may want to adapt the examples to match more closely the needs of your students. Activities are typically generic in format; you should be able to modify them to meet the needs of different ages and abilities. You can try them with a small group or the whole class. Once an activity is completed, evaluate its effectiveness in developing children's mathematical understanding, always bearing in mind the responses of your students, especially those new to calculator use.

As you and your students become more confident in working with calculators, you may wish to integrate the calculator into your everyday mathematics teaching. Work with calculators should form part of normal classroom activity rather than being a special reward or mode of busywork for children who have completed their regular assignments.

Be prepared to learn along with your students, as together you explore the use of the calculator as a powerful tool in your mathematics classroom.

Calculators and the Classroom: Questions Teachers Ask

▼ 1. What is the best type of calculator for elementary and middle school students?

Simple four-function calculators (for adding, subtracting, multiplying, and dividing) are used throughout the elementary and middle school years. Almost all of the activities in this book can be done with a four-function calculator. Most educational publishers' catalogs offer a range of models. Selection criteria should be based on the needs of your class and the work you wish to undertake. Possible considerations include:

- ◆ number and function keys that are appropriately sized and spaced for young users (not too small or close together)
- ◆ keys that have a definite feel when pressed
- ◆ an easy-to-read display
- ◆ constant-function capability
- ◆ solar-powered operation
- ◆ a sturdy plastic case
- ◆ affordability

Older children might require advanced-function calculators offering additional capabilities, such as:

- ◆ computation with fractions
- ◆ use of order-of-operations logic
- ◆ features to develop place-value ideas
- ◆ conversion from fractions to decimals and percentages
- ◆ use of indices such as squaring

▼ 2. What are the major differences and similarities among the various types and models of calculators?

Calculators generally fall into one of three categories.

1. *Four-function calculators*. The term "four-function" is somewhat misleading, because these simple calculators tend to have square root and percentage keys along with memory options, which takes them well beyond the four basic operations of addition, subtraction, multiplication, and division. These calculators are appropriate for younger children and are most commonly found in elementary schools.

2. *Advanced-function calculators*. Calculators in this category go beyond the basic features to include the ability to work with fractions, do integer division, and fix and round the number of decimal places in the answer. Various models of this type are available in business supply stores. These calculators are seen as suitable for older children, for example those in grades six to eight, but again are not required for the majority of activities in this book.

3. *Graphing calculators*. These are highly sophisticated calculators that allow functions to be graphed, provide solutions to algebraic equations, and accommodate statistical problems. They are appropriate for advanced-level math students in high school and college.

Rule of Order

Aside from their more limited capabilities, four-function calculators differ from advanced-function calculators in the way that they handle calculations. Four-function calculators, which use arithmetic logic, perform calculations in the order in which they are entered. Advanced-function calculators (scientific calculators are an example of these) are programmed to use the mathematically correct rule of order in operations. This is an issue only when a calculation involves a mix of operations, such as addition and multiplication. For example, in solving the equation 2 + 3 x 4, a four-function calculator would perform the calculation in the order in which it was entered; if entered as shown here, a result of 20 would be produced. By contrast, calculators that employ the rule of order will abide by a set hierarchy of operations, tackling the various parts of mixed equations as follows:

1. Bracketed elements
2. Indices (e.g., squares and cubes)
3. Multiplication and division

4. Addition and subtraction

In the example 2 + 3 **x** 4, an advanced-function calculator would solve the multiplication part of the equation first, then the addition, producing the mathematically correct answer of 14.

Rather than discourage the use of simple calculators that use arithmetic logic, teachers can use this functional limitation as a point of discussion with older children. Children can be shown that calculators are not infallible and may at times produce incorrect results if the user is not aware of basic mathematical principles, such as the rule of order, in working with them.

The Constant Function

Perhaps the most useful calculator function for teaching purposes is the constant function. Here the calculator supports children's conception of relationships and patterns in math. This function is utilized in many of the activities in Section 2. Depending on the model and make of the calculator, varying sequences of keystrokes are used to enable this feature. However, three elements are required: a start number, an operation (+, −, **x**, ÷), and a step number. For example, using the constant function on the calculator to show counting by fives would involve the following steps:

1. Clear the display.
2. Enter the start number; for example, 0 (in many cases this will already be shown on the calculator).
3. Enter the operation; for example, addition.
4. Enter the step number; for example, 5.

In order to see the pattern the user will need to press the equal key. Each time the equal key is pressed, the number in the display will increase by five.

Any variation of starting number, step number, and operation can be used. For example, to count back in sevens from ninety-nine, the user would do the following:

1. Clear the display.
2. Enter the start number; for example, 99.
3. Enter the operation; for example, subtraction.
4. Enter the step number; for example, 7.

The user would then press the equal key repeatedly to see the emerging pattern in the display.

Rounding and Truncating

Input the equation 1 ÷ 3 = into the calculator and note the recurring decimal (0.3333333) shown on the display. Multiply this number by 3. Logic suggests that the result will be 1, but some calculators will give 0.9999999. Simple four-function calculators have difficulty handling recurring decimals, because they continue forever. To overcome this problem, advanced-function calculators are programmed to do one of two things: (1) truncate, or cut off, the number or (2) round the number.

Slight differences will occur between calculators that are programmed to truncate and those programmed to round. For example, the nine-digit answer to 2.0006 x 3.0003 is 6.00240018, but a calculator programmed to truncate would give an answer of 6.0024001, whereas a calculator that rounds would produce an answer of 6.0024002. The rounded result is more accurate in this case. The differences are only minor, however, and such a degree of inaccuracy is generally acceptable in calculations performed at the elementary and middle school levels.

Working with Fractions

Many advanced-function calculators allow fractions to be entered in the way they would be written. Some of the newer calculators incorporate a two-line display that allows a fraction to be viewed with the numerator above the denominator. Fractions are entered into four-function calculators using the following sequence: numerator (top number) divided by denominator (bottom number). This process converts the fraction into a decimal that is then used to complete the operation; for example, $\frac{1}{3}$ = 1 ÷ 3 or 0.3333333.

Memory

One of the least used and yet most powerful features found on the calculator is the memory function. Using the memory keys, numbers can be stored for reuse in calculations. Note that the actions of storing, retrieving, and using numbers stored in memory vary among the different makes and models of calculators. Most calculators have M+ and M– keys, which can be used to add or subtract numbers shown in the display to whatever is stored in memory. To check or retrieve the number stored in a calculator's memory, press the memory recall (often shown as MRC) key. In most cases, the default number stored in memory is zero. The M– key can also be used to subtract the number shown in the display from the number stored in memory. The memory function is extremely useful when performing repetitive calculations (for example, 143 x

7 =, 143 x 14 =, 143 x 21 =, 143 x 28 =, 143 x 35 =, and so on). In this case it saves time by allowing the user to press one key rather than three. Also, it reduces the chance of pressing incorrect keys, allowing the user to focus on the pattern being generated rather than on pressing the correct keys.

Clearing Keys

An understanding of the way in which the display is cleared is important in the efficient use of calculators. Again, makes and models vary, but most calculators allow for both clearing of the entire display—usually via the clear (C), all clear (AC), or On/C key—and of only the last entry inputted, usually via a key marked CE (clear entry). Children often make keying errors when using a calculator, and often clear the entire calculation and start from the beginning rather than clear the last entry that was made. The CE key allows minor mistakes to be rectified without having to repeat the entire calculation. The clear or all clear keys on most calculators tend to also clear information stored in memory. Time spent familiarizing oneself with the way in which different makes and models of calculators clear the display can save time and minimize frustration.

▼ 3. Should all students in a class use the same model calculator?

When teachers first begin using calculators in the classroom, all children should use the same model, to minimize confusion and facilitate learning about basic features and functions. However, with older children who are familiar with calculators, the differences between makes and models and their varying levels of functional capability can be useful in supporting inquiry-based teaching and learning. We also think that it is important for children to have access to calculators capable of more advanced functions as their mathematical ability increases. Moreover, we feel that children's technological literacy is an important educational goal; in this respect, teachers should encourage students' exposure to the wide range of calculators they will encounter in the real world.

▼ 4. What is number sense, and what role can calculators play in its development?

According to McIntosh, Reys, and Reys (1997), number sense is defined as "a person's general understanding of numbers and operations along with the ability and inclination to use this understanding in flexible ways to make mathematical judgments and to develop useful and efficient strategies for dealing with numbers and operations" (322). Number sense refers to more than mental computation and estimation. It involves flexibility and creativity with numbers as well as the confidence to use them in a variety of ways. This is quite different from a view of numbers as involving a set of learned procedures applied without respect to context or efficiency.

Calculators encourage children's mathematical exploration because they allow for efficient handling of numbers and data. The calculator enables children to complete calculations more quickly than would be possible using paper-and-pencil methods, affording children more time and energy to see relationships and patterns and grasp underlying concepts.

The calculator is also useful in helping children to think about numbers in meaningful ways. If children can see numbers in terms of patterns and relationships, they are more likely to use numbers flexibly to meet the needs of various situations. The ability to observe, predict, and test patterns is fundamental to the development of problem-solving strategies. When they are engaged in this type of activity, it may be said that children are "working as mathematicians."

The development of number sense requires that children do mental computation and perform estimation. Used as a teaching and learning aid, the calculator can also help children acquire these skills and strategies.

It is important that children be fully engaged in any computation they perform. Students often utilize standard written algorithms without thinking about the calculation at hand or the numbers involved. In fact, standard written methods were designed so that one did not have to think. To encourage their active participation in performing a calculation, children should be encouraged to examine a problem carefully in order to decide on an appropriate computational approach.

Number sense also extends to the checking and reflection stage. If an exact answer is required, children with developed number sense will be able to first make an estimation, which can then be used to check the reasonableness of the answer they arrive at through calculation. While performing the calculation, children should be alert to see whether separate parts of the equation make sense. Checking a calculation may also involve repeating the problem in a different order. Experience or common sense alone may alert a student with number sense that an answer is incorrect. For example, when answering the question, "How many buses will be needed to transport a group of 150 students, if each bus holds 30 students?" common sense should tell a child that 50 buses is an incorrect answer. This experiential approach to checking is possible only if the context of the question is familiar or realistic. Children may also apply various intuitive ideas as an approach to checking. For example, children who through experience are aware that multiplying two even numbers will always produce an even result will be quick to spot an error if they complete the multiplication of two even numbers only to find the result is odd.

▼ 5. What is "appropriate" or "sensible" calculator use?

Appropriate or sensible calculator use aids in the development of children's number sense. Like any piece of equipment, the calculator can be put to productive or counterproductive use. Complicating the situation is that interpretations of sensible calculator use vary widely among parents and teachers. Some feel that calculators can and should be used all the time, while others advocate restricting use to certain well-defined activities or to students of a certain age or level of ability.

In explaining sensible or appropriate use, it is helpful to point out practices that are clearly *not* sensible, such as:

◆ using the calculator to make words on the display, by inputting numbers that look like letters when the calculator is turned upside down
◆ using the calculator for calculations that can be easily and more efficiently completed mentally
◆ using the calculator only to check work that was completed with pencil and paper
◆ keying in textbook problems to practice standard computational methods

Inappropriate Calculator Use

Busywork, Drill, and Practice

The mindless keying in of endless exercises from textbooks certainly meets the criteria of busywork. Even special calculator activities can degenerate into busywork without proper teacher intervention. As Dick (1988) stated, "Mechanically grinding through paper-and-pencil computations would not appear to lend itself to insights about arithmetic any more than mechanically moving the beads on an abacus, manipulating a slide rule, or operating a calculator" (39).

Checking Work

This is perhaps the most common misuse of calculators in the elementary and middle school. Johnson (1985) called the practice of checking work with a calculator an "abuse" of this tool, asking, "Why use the calculator to check, when it is usually the best device for performing the calculations in the first place?" (15). Reys and Reys (1987) expanded on this thinking, maintaining that using the calculator only for checking work does not reflect real-world practice and implies that calculator use is a form of "cheating."

Indiscriminate Use

When calculators are used indiscriminately, as for example when the teacher is merely following a textbook recommendation to use them with a particular unit, mathematics instruction will suffer. Duffin (1994), who reviewed the Calculator Aware Number project in the United Kingdom, commented, "[T]he calculator does not inhibit thinking; it only does so when it is introduced without care to use it properly" (28). Koop (1979) noted, "[T]he worst way to use a calculator is to use it for the sake of using it. Calculators should be used as a natural part of the mathematics lesson" (7).

Sensible Calculator Use

A common feature of inappropriate calculator use is that little or no thinking by children is required. What distinguishes sensible calculator use from inappropriate use is that, with the former, children are stimulated to think about mathematics and numbers; used sensibly, calculators promote mathematical understanding. Whether or not children's thought processes are engaged is a key element in determining if a particular calculator use is sensible or not.

Children faced with a problem requiring a computation should be able to decide for themselves if the use of a calculator is appropriate. They should be able to examine a calculation, consider their options, and justify their choice of employing:

- mental methods
- pencil-and-paper methods
- a computer
- a calculator
- a combination of the above

Many children are unable to make a sensible choice between the various computational alternatives because they have been taught to use only one with any proficiency—the standard written algorithm.

Critics of calculators in the classroom argue that students overrely on these tools and become lazy in their practice of mathematics. However, sensible use of calculators develops mathematical proficiency; as students further their understanding of strategies and concepts, they realize that it is often more efficient to use their head than to reach for a calculator. Sensible use, therefore, relies on number sense as much as it promotes the development of it.

▼ 6. What issues of classroom management should be addressed regarding calculator use?

The following questions can help teachers make decisions about classroom management with respect to calculator use.

Will each child have a calculator, much in the same way that they have other basic tools, such as a ruler?

Will children be able to use calculators as and when they wish, or will the teacher determine when it is appropriate to use them?

Will calculators be easily available or will they have to be distributed as needed?

Is there a school, class, personal, or group set of calculators?

Where will calculators be kept in the classroom?

We would recommend that children have "easy access" to calculators so that they have the option of using them and do not have to disturb the teacher or the other members of the class to do so. Calculators should be available on students' desks or within easy reach of their assigned seats. Children would have to justify their computational choice and take responsibility for using the calculator appropriately and sensibly, and teachers would have the option of regulating calculator use with respect to particular activities. Easy access also prevents a novelty effect from developing around calculator use, as calculators come to be seen as everyday classroom equipment.

▼ 7. Should schools develop policies on calculator use?

A carefully thought-out and articulated policy on calculator use is very important in a school. The following questions have been designed to assist in the construction of such a policy. Not all the questions need to be specifically addressed; rather, they are intended to form the basis of a healthy debate. The aim should be to produce a short document as part of an overall school mathematics policy.

Who should be given access to calculators?

Will calculators be available
◆ all the time?
◆ at the request of the students?
◆ when the teacher decides that they are appropriate?

Should the school supply class sets of calculators? If so, how would these calculators be stored?

Should children provide their own calculators?

Should the make and model of calculator be specified?

Will calculators be allowed in test situations? When might access to calculators in test circumstances be limited or obligatory?

Will children of different ages have different calculators?

How does the school policy relate to national and state principles and standards?

How will the use of calculators be linked to other areas of number work?

What will be emphasized or deemphasized in mathematics teaching if children are allowed easy access to calculators? For example, how will the balance between estimation, basic facts, mental computation, and written algorithms be altered?

How will the policy be communicated with parents?

Will specific lessons on calculator use be given? Will children be taught specific calculator skills?

How will calculators be utilized in other areas of the curriculum?

How will calculators be used as a teaching tool and a computational tool?

How will tasks change as a result of children being allowed easy access to calculators?

How will calculator use be evaluated and monitored?

▼ 8. What are the principles of good classroom practice with respect to calculators?

Most curriculum documents offer recommendations for good practice with respect to calculator use. The thinking emerging from research findings is that all children should have access to calculators and be able to choose if and when they are to use them, as well as to explain or justify that choice.

Another main principle for good classroom practice is that calculators be fully integrated into mathematics teaching and learning. Tasks employing the calculator:

- provide children with mathematical insight
- further development of children's number sense
- involve children in discussion and explanation
- encourage children to consider more efficient ways to carry out a calculation
- encourage children to ask "What if" questions
- enhance learning in mental mathematics, estimation, problem solving, investigation, place value, and pattern.

The following questions may help teachers in planning, adapting, or appraising calculator activities for use in the classroom.

What roles do mental computation and estimation play?

How does the task take into account the range of abilities found in the classroom?

How might the task be extended or adapted?

How might the information gained from children participating in the tasks be used for assessment purposes?

What aspects of mathematics or number sense is involved?

One of the fundamental questions teachers should ask themselves when considering a task is, "What is the purpose of the calculator in this situation?" We have also found it useful to check tasks against the following list of questions:

Can the calculator do aspects of the task more quickly?
Can the calculator do aspects of the task more efficiently?
Can the calculator do aspects of the task that could not be done without it?

▼ 9. What role should the calculator play in mathematics teaching?

Teachers wishing to introduce calculators into their classrooms often have difficulty seeing how calculators can fit into a balanced mathematics program. It is important that calculators be integrated into a mathematics program that emphasizes a variety of computational approaches and strategies, in an environment promoting number sense. Calculator use should not be contrived but natural; children should be able to make use of these tools as they see fit. In order for teachers and parents to feel comfortable with this approach, calculator use should be appropriate and sensible—that is, based on the development of number sense.

▼ 10. What is an integrated approach to calculator use, and how can it be implemented?

One of the great strengths of the calculator is that it aids in children's understanding of mathematical concepts and relationships. At the planning stage of a mathematics program, teachers identify concepts that students will be expected to understand. It is at this point that calculator use can be considered as a means of supporting the proposed learning, much in the way one might utilize various educational tools and resources. One might seek opportunities for children to use the calculator to generate data quickly, explore large numbers, complete tedious calculations, and investigate numbers in a variety of ways. A calculator is useful not only in supporting mathematics learning but also in other areas of the curriculum. Science experiments, for example, produce data that can be combined and analyzed quickly with the aid of a calculator.

For the calculator to be accepted as supporting the curriculum rather than as something to be used after the required mathematics work has been completed, clear links between calculator use and the curriculum must be established. These links can be made to number work in the elementary school, but more is required than simply using the calculator to complete a set of sums. We do not propose, for example, replacing traditional pencil-and-paper sums with more difficult sums to be completed with a calculator. Such an activity requires minimal mathematical thinking on the part of the child.

Table 1–1, although by no means comprehensive, is included as a guide to how calculator use may be integrated into the mathematics curriculum. The table should not be viewed as a list to be checkmarked each time a cal-

Grade Level	Aspects of Calculator Use
K–2	◆ key recognition: 0–9 ◆ key recognition: +, −, x, =, ÷ ◆ key recognition: clear ◆ matching written and display styles for numbers ◆ use of constant key ◆ read display ◆ change an incorrect entry ◆ use calculator-related language
3–4	◆ use the estimate-calculate-check rubric ◆ interpret the decimal part of an answer; ◆ aware of rounding and truncating aspects of calculators
5–8	◆ use of % key ◆ use of memory ◆ use of toggle key (+/−) ◆ possible development from a fraction calculator to a simple graphing machine. ◆ use of negative numbers ◆ use of square root key ◆ use of iterative strategies ◆ use of the correct key sequence for calculations with more than one operation ◆ select whether to use mental, written, or calculator approach

Table 1–1. Aspects of Calculator Use

culator is employed in the classroom, and the placement of items within the table does not imply a hierarchy of skills. This becomes most evident when a topic such as "reading numbers" is considered. Although obvious curricular links to place value can be made, the topic is revisited at various times throughout elementary and middle school mathematics instruction.

▼ 11. Should lessons focus specifically on calculator use?

It may be necessary to focus specifically on the calculator when it is being introduced in the classroom, in order to teach children about basic functions and the practices of sensible use. For students familiar with calculators and in classrooms utilizing an integrated approach, isolated lessons on calculator use should not be necessary.

An example of an integrated approach, whereby a specific calculator skill is embedded in an activity designed to teach mathematics content, concerns the use of the memory keys. When looking for patterns in the 99 times table, children can be taught to use the memory key or the constant function on the calculator; quick performance of these calculations reveals patterns that aid in the development of number sense. Similarly, instruction about the memory and constant functions could occur as part of the activity. Children can also be encouraged to determine how a percentage calculation would be performed on different models of calculators and then compare these methods to the standard pencil-and-paper approach. This could lead to a discussion of individual methods of mental calculation.

When planning activities, teachers should ask themselves two important questions:

How will the calculator be used so that specific features, such as the constant function, are taught and learned?

How will the task incorporate the exploration of an idea or the solving of a problem?

▼ 12. What are the basic calculator skills that children need to learn?

Research and curriculum documents have identified the following as basic calculator skills:

◆ Employment of appropriate mental checking strategies, such as estimation and approximation
◆ Ability to gauge appropriateness of calculator-derived answers
◆ Ability to read and write (enter) numbers on the calculator
◆ Efficient and effective use of function keys (memory, square root, percentage, etc.)

- Knowledge of how to interpret the display, using strategies such as rounding
- Knowledge of order of operations and how to apply it
- Ability to make decisions among mental, written, and calculator approaches
- Ability to calculate with fractions in the absence of a fraction function
- Ability to use the constant function:
  - to count forward
  - to count backward
  - with multiples and divisors
  - to do repeated addition and subtraction with powers of ten
- Understanding of how to use the calculator sensibly for various non-school purposes

▼ 13. What activities can be used to introduce calculators into the classroom?

Depending on the age of the children, a number of general activities have been found useful for introducing calculators into the classroom; these include Tell Me, described in Section 2.

Different children believe different things about the calculator. Many teachers consider it a good idea to first find out exactly what it is that children know and believe about calculators. This gives useful information as to a possible starting point, and as to any misconceptions about the calculator that children may hold. Some children in the classroom may already have developed a variety of skills on the calculator, whereas others are possibly being introduced to the calculator for the very first time. Activities that identify and acknowledge these differences are important and useful starting points.

The observation of number patterns can help children develop intuition with respect to checking answers. For example, children who have explored multiplication with two-digit numbers are aware of patterns that occur with these types of calculations, and know what types of results to expect when performing them. For example, when multiplying a two-digit number by a two-digit number, children will observe that the result is always a three-digit or four-digit number.

▼ 14. What strategies can maximize learning with calculators?

Activities should be adapted as required to better fit the needs of children. One general way of doing this is to ask questions about the task using the phrase, "What if . . . ?" Another way is to ask children to find more than one way to solve the problem. These questions allow children as well as teachers to explore activities more fully. The following activity serves as an example.

Restricted Key Problems
Math goal: Children will use their knowledge of number relationships to develop flexible ways of using numbers.

Grades: 6–8

Materials: Calculator for each child; pencil and paper for recording.

Activity: Tell children that they can use only these keys on the calculator, but that each key may be used more than once:

$$\boxed{4} \quad \boxed{3} \quad \boxed{-} \quad \boxed{\times} \quad \boxed{=}$$

Ask them to explain how, using a combination of these keys, they would arrive at the following results.

Number	Keys pressed and order of pressing
9	
12	
6	
5	

The activity can be extended using the "What if . . . ?" technique. For example:

> What if the keys to press were 3 and 5?
> What if the operation to be used was + rather than – ?

Students could also be challenged to find more than one way (or all possible ways) to arrive at a particular result (e.g., 9 = 3 x 3; 9 = 4 x 3 – 3).

Teaching Note

The above example serves to illustrate that effective tasks may be adapted and extended by changing one of the parameters or asking slightly different questions. To gain the most from these tasks, however, children need to be given the opportunity to:

◆ explore the situation
◆ discuss what they are doing
◆ explain what they have found

▼ 15. How can calculators help children learn basic number facts?

The argument is often made that children should learn their basic number facts before they are permitted to use calculators, or that use of calculators eliminates the need for children to learn basic facts.

We think that in the age of calculators and computers, it is especially important that children have basic fact recall, and that calculators can aid in children's learning of such facts by furthering their ability to conceptualize and model. Calculators can help children see where the connections and relationships are, enabling them to develop deeper understanding.

▼ 16. How can calculators be used to teach about specific mathematical content?

Used as a teaching and learning aid, the calculator can be a useful tool in developing specific mathematical content. For example, with respect to place value, always a difficult concept for children to grasp, the calculator can support children's understanding of:

◆ the size and value of numbers
◆ ordering by size
◆ the value of numerical place
◆ how the place-value system develops from left to right (i.e., it grows by a factor of ten for each column), and right to left (it decreases by a factor of ten for each column)
◆ the effect of adding or subtracting ten or a hundred

19

◆ the effect of multiplying or dividing by ten or a hundred

Other content areas in which the calculator supports learning include:

◆ number patterns
◆ averages
◆ fraction, decimal, and percentage relationships

▼ 17. How can calculators be used with the math textbook?

Textbooks reflect various levels of calculator inclusion. Some contain few or no recommendations; others include specific calculator activities; still others allow for integrated calculator use. Teachers should determine the extent to which the textbook promotes sensible, appropriate use of calculators, and plan calculator instruction with the textbook accordingly.

The calculator can further children's understanding of the instruction contained in any math textbook, even those not intended to support calculator use. Textbook activities are typically closed in nature, requiring the application of a specific procedure. With calculators, however, they can be opened up to require children to think about numbers and relationships and explore underlying concepts and patterns.

▼ 18. How can calculators help children learn about fractions?

Calculators can be used to convert fractions to decimals and so help children gain an idea of the relative sizes of fractions. Using calculators to find equivalent fractions can also further children's conceptual understanding.

Fraction calculators and calculators with fraction-manipulation capabilities are now widely available. Some models allow the user to key in fractions as they are traditionally written, with numerator and denominator separated by a horizontal bar.

Whether one is using whole numbers or fractions, the principles of calculator use remain the same. That is, the calculator is used to enhance children's number sense. Fractions are notoriously difficult for children to understand; failure to achieve understanding in this area can lead to the development in children of negative attitudes to mathematics and of themselves as mathematicians. Calculator activities and tasks are developed to support children's thinking about fractional numbers and their relationships, enabling them to conceptualize fractions and gain understanding.

▼ 19. How can calculators aid in children's use of real-world data?

Children can use calculators to compute large sums and work with real and complex data. Such information is typically beyond children's ability to handle unaided. Textbook problems, designed to be accessible to children, typically use contrived contexts and data; by contrast, real-world data is typically messy and measurements often take the form of difficult fractions and decimals, which can be inaccessible to children without the use of calculators. Moreover, calculators enable children to work with large numbers and complex data quickly and efficiently, allowing them to record and interpret information that would otherwise be overwhelming to them, and to gain understanding of the underlying concepts.

▼ 20. How can calculators be used to set challenges and devise problems for children?

The calculator is an effective teaching tool that can be used in imaginative ways to challenge children to solve problems while learning mathematical concepts and becoming accustomed to sensible calculator use. Activities throughout this book adopt a problem-solving stance. Again, a fundamental question to ask when creating calculator-related tasks for children is, "Will children be required to think about numbers as they solve this problem?"

Section 2 offers challenging tasks for children to undertake with the help of a calculator. Many are generic in style (for example, Targets and Broken Keys) and may be adapted for use with different numbers and for different children.

▼ 21. How can children's learning with calculators be assessed?

Assessment activities should require students to do more than just produce an answer on their calculator. They should be asked to record their key presses or explain what procedure they followed and why. Many of the activities offered in Section 2 are suitable for assessment purposes, as they engage children in thinking about numbers and drawing conclusions from observations and solutions. Such conclusions can provide valuable insight into students' mathematical understanding and levels of competence.

▼ 22. Should calculators be allowed during tests?

The answer here depends on why you are testing and what information you wish to obtain. If you wish to know if students can recall number relationships, then allowing them to use calculators defeats the object of the exercise. If, on the other hand, you wish to see how a child approaches and solves a problem, then the use of calculators should be an option. Obviously, if you are looking to assess students' ability to use a calculator, then the calculator is a necessary part of the assessment.

It seems logical that if a calculator is available to children when they are learning mathematics, it should play a role in the assessment of their understanding. Tests should be formulated, however, to accommodate a calculator-available situation. For example, asking children to solve the equation 27 x 4 with a calculator available provides limited information about children's understanding of multiplication, as all that they are required to do is key in the numbers correctly. However, a test could ask them to find four different ways to calculate 27 x 4 and then describe what they have done.

▼ 23. How can activities be adapted to meet the needs of a particular class?

All classes reflect a range of abilities, and offering tasks and activities to match the abilities of all children can be a challenge. The use of the calculator as a teaching and learning aid alongside a variety of tasks is one way to resolve the problem.

We have already discussed setting a core task and asking children for different ways to solve the problem. With any task, it is important that it can be made easier or more difficult to suit the requirements of children. Open-ended tasks allow children to set their own level of difficulty and complexity in answering.

Activities offered in Section 2 illustrate how typical textbook tasks may be changed from a closed to an open format to match the abilities of a class. Tasks may also be recycled to match varying levels of ability and different ages of children.

▼ 24. Can calculators help children with learning difficulties?

When children are unable to perform a calculation using pencil and paper, a calculator can be a liberating tool, enabling them to produce an accurate answer in a short amount of time. In this sense, children achieve success rather than failure—a most important aspect of developing a positive attitude to mathematics.

Calculators are a useful aid to children with learning difficulties because for many children they are a powerful motivator and offer a new beginning. The calculator can also act as a challenge to children's thinking and possible misconceptions. The Wipeout activity described in Section 2, for example, provokes children's thinking about place value.

The calculator can be a great motivator for all children, and offers variety and a change of pace from traditional teaching methods. This can be helpful to children who experience difficulty with mathematics and suffer from low self-esteem as a result. Too often children with difficulties are faced with a repetition of the same content and teaching methods that have already failed them. Calculators can offer an exciting new tool that enables them to experience success.

▼ 25. What are the most common parental concerns surrounding calculator use and how can they be addressed?

A widespread perception holds that calculators in the classroom have replaced children's thinking about numbers, calculations, and mathematics in general. One way to show that calculators require children to think about mathematics and are a vital part of developing number sense is to invite parents and community leaders into the classroom to see children using calculators in sensible ways. Explaining to parents that calculators are part of a balanced program that emphasizes mental computation as a valid computational choice will also reassure parents that calculators are not used as a substitute for thinking in the classroom but rather to promote it.

Letters sent home with homework tasks, explaining the role of the calculator in activities designed to develop children's understanding of numbers or to identify relationships and strategies would also be useful. Such letters should emphasize your view of the calculator as a teaching and learning aid aimed at improving children's mathematical ability and developing their number sense.

Parent evening workshops are another way to try to inform parents and the local community of your aims for using calculators in the classroom. Activities involving the children that show sensible calculator use are essential to alleviate parental fears of mindless key pushing. Activities such as Broken Keys, Restricted Keys, and Four Steps to Zero are helpful ones to use at a parent evening, to show that sensible calculator activities require children (and adults) to think about numbers and their relationships and patterns.

Most parental concerns arise from a fear of children losing their ability to calculate and also from a lack of understanding of the role of the calculator in elementary and middle school mathematics. Although there is considerable evidence to indicate that sensible use of calculators does not reduce children's ability to perform written and mental calculation, parents can be wary of or ignorant of research findings.

Experience suggests that direct contact with parents, including by inviting them into the classroom, is the best way to address their concerns about teaching and learning methods. It is important that a dialogue be maintained between the school and the parents. A well-developed school policy on calculator use will assist in directing much of this dialogue.

Myths Surrounding Calculator Use

Children Who Use Calculators Are Mentally Lazy

This comment is often made when adults observe children using calculators to complete trivial calculations. It is true that when first given a calculator, a novelty effect takes over and children use the calculator for just about everything. This effect eventually wears off, however, and with clear guidance from the teacher, children soon become discerning as to when it is appropriate to use a calculator and when it is not.

Standards Have Fallen Since the Introduction of Calculators into Schools

This comment is typically made in reference to a teenager who has trouble calculating change at a cash register. Most teenagers are the product of a mathematics education that focused on written computation. Calculators, if they were used at all during these teenagers' elementary education, were probably restricted to checking answers, trivial exercises, and games. They cannot, therefore, be blamed for low math aptitude. There has always been a segment of the population who has struggled with mathematics, not because of the use of calculators but because they were bored and did not understand what they were being taught and how the mathematics they were learning applied to the real world. In studies of the effect of calculators on achievement, results have indicated no detrimental effects on children's mathematical ability (Hembree and Dessart 1986; 1992).

Because of Calculators, Children Are No Longer Required to Learn Basic Math

Calculators are not designed to replace the learning of basic number facts. The basic number facts are more essential than ever, given the availability of calculators. Number sense is required for estimation and mental computation and must always be employed to monitor calculations performed with the aid of calculators.

With Calculators, Children Don't Have to Think for Themselves

Try the following calculation with the aid of a calculator:

How long is a million seconds?

In order to answer this question, the user must know how many seconds there are in a minute, minutes in an hour, hours in a day, and so on. Without this prior knowledge, the person cannot start to solve the problem. Even with this knowledge, the person needs to determine which operation is required, complete the sequence of calculations, and determine the result shown on the display. This helps to illustrate that calculators do not think, and the user has to apply basic knowledge of relationships and facts.

When calculators are used sensibly, a great deal of thinking has to take place. All activities suggested in this book require children to think about numbers and context in working with calculators.

Calculators Are Not Used in the Real World

Business demands that employees be able to problem solve, think, and work as a team. All of these elements are addressed in a balanced mathematics program. Written computation first gained prominence during the industrial revolution, when factory owners needed clerks who were able to calculate wages, stock production, and profits. The role of the clerk has changed as a result of the technological revolution. Today, calculations are performed on spreadsheets or with the aid of a computer or a calculator. Employers expect that employees will use the most efficient means of calculation available, which in most cases will be a spreadsheet or calculator.

Calculators Inhibit Children's Mathematical Growth

This argument is based on the notion that children should learn the basic number facts prior to being given access to calculators. We suggest that when calculators are used properly, they can be used to teach the basics. The calculator's constant feature, especially, can be used to advantage when teaching the basics. Delaying the introduction of calculators can introduce a novelty effect, leading to children's overuse of calculators. This can be avoided if calculators are seen as a natural part of the school environment from the time children begin school.

Calculators Are Too Expensive for Many Schools and Families

The costs of calculators have fallen to the point where they are within the price range of most families. Calculators of a quality suited to elementary school cost approximately ten dollars. Less expensive versions—less than the price of a hamburger—are readily available.

▼ 26. Where can I find other sources of calculator activities?

Many calculator manufacturers provide Web sites that offer activities for calculator use. Still other mathematics sites contain lessons and tasks submitted by teachers. A word of caution is offered: Many suggested activities fall well outside what we have described as sensible use of calculators. Often they are no more than low-level busywork or activities that promote trivial, non-thinking uses of the calculator.

One of the richest sources of activities is your classroom math textbook. Although textbook tasks are typically closed and limited in nature, by adapting the question or task to allow for open-ended exploration with calculators children's thinking and learning about mathematics can be extended and advanced.

SECTION TWO

Calculator Activities for the Classroom

In the activities that follow, calculator use supports the development of children's number sense, requiring them to think about particular contexts and situations. The activities reflect various levels of calculator involvement, but all of them require children to engage, explore, and explain: Students are expected to engage in the task, explore the mathematical concept underlying it, and explain their results.

It is crucial that students reflect on and discuss the activities and what they have learned in working through them. The activities by themselves have limited value. It is only at the point of reflection and explanation that children can make connections and achieve new or deeper understanding.

As previously stated, the activities offered here lend themselves to adaptation, development, and recycling, so that teachers can more closely address the needs and abilities of their students. In developing these exercises, teachers will build a useful store of resource activities for calculator use in the classroom.

▼ SAME EQUATION, DIFFERENT ANSWER

Math Goal

Children will understand that keying in equations using the same sequence of numbers on different types of calculators may produce two different answers. Advanced-function calculators tend to use an order-of-operations approach, whereby multiplication and division operations are completed before addition and subtraction. Simple four-function calculators require the user to apply order of operations when inputting mixed-operation equations. Keying in an equation as it appears on the page could result in a wrong answer.

order of operations

Grades
6–8

Materials
Two calculators for each pair of children—a simple four-function model and an advanced-function calculator that uses order-of-operations logic. (Before beginning the activity, check—by inputting an appropriate equation, such as the one below—that the calculators give different answers. Whether they use order-of-operations logic is not always apparent from looking at them.) Paper and pencil for recording.

Activity
The purpose of this activity is to promote discussion among children. Often, children believe that an answer provided by a calculator is infallible. The activity causes conflict or doubt in the children's minds, and the discussion will help to challenge this belief.

Ask students to answer the following equation:

$3 + 4 \times 5 =$

Have them enter this equation into both calculators and write down what is shown on both displays. The four-function calculator will give an answer of 35, while the advanced-function calculator will produce the correct answer of 23.

The reason for this—which you can explain to the children—is that the first calculator solves the equation in the order in which it is keyed in; that is, the numbers and symbols are read from left to right, with the addition operation preceding the multiplication:

$(3 + 4) \times 5$

giving an answer of 35. The second calculator reads the equation using the order-of-operations rule, as

$3 + (4 \times 5)$

producing the correct answer, 23. In this case the calculator performs the multiplication operation before the addition.

Have the children explore other strings of numbers on the calculators and note their responses using a chart like this one, which shows sample equations:

Problem	Answer on four-function calculator	Answer on advanced-function calculator
2 + 3 + 6		
2 x 3 + 7		
7 + 2 x 3		
20 – 10 ÷ 2		
26 + 5 – 7 x 3		
2 + 8 – 3 x 4 ÷ 2		

Discuss with children why certain combinations of operations result in the same answer on both types of calculator.

Extension

Children will need several different models of calculators. Ask children to categorize these calculators by whether they use order of operations or not.

Teaching Notes

While the purpose of this activity is to promote discussion and understanding about order of operations, we would not encourage the development of an acronym, such as BIMDAS (Brackets, Indices, Multiplication, Division, Addition, and Subtraction), to describe the order in which parts of the calculation should occur. For example, BIMDAS implies that multiplication should be done before division and addition before subtraction. In reality, however, if multiplication and division were in the same calculation, they would be completed from left to right as they occur in the calculation.

▼ MAKE YOUR CHOICE

Math Goal

Children will think about a calculation before they undertake it and identify the most appropriate and effective method to use.

Grades
3–5; 6–8

Materials
Calculator and paper for recording for each child.

Activity
Ask the children to study the following chart (or one like it shown on the board) and respond to the Extensions below.

Problem	Method for calculating (mental, calculator, pencil-and-paper)	Reason for choice
14 + 21		
79 + 42		
7 x 9		
20 x 40		
600 ÷ 30		
400 ÷ 25		

Extensions

1. Choose two equations for which you think the best way to answer is by using mental mathematics.
2. Choose two equations for which you would use a pencil-and-paper calculation.
3. Choose two equations that are best answered by using a calculator.

Children must then explain their reasoning in choosing a method for each equation.

Teaching Notes
Discuss the choices made by the children and ask them to explain why they

selected a particular method for computation. Children's responses give teachers insight into their thought processes, their level of confidence in selecting calculating methods, and their possible misunderstandings. These features can then be addressed in future lessons as part of the process of approaching equations and of sensible calculator use.

▼ WIPEOUT

Math Goal

Children will understand that in a number containing multiple digits, the position of the number (whether it is in the ones, tens, hundreds, thousands, etc., column) affects its value or size—that is, its face value may be different from its place value.

Grades

3–5

Materials

One calculator for each pair of children.

Activity

One member of the pair enters a three- to eight-digit number, without zeroes or repeated digits, into the display of the calculator. The other student must then remove any digit from the display using a subtraction operation, replacing it with zero, without changing any of the other digits. For example, if the first student enters the number 12345678 into the calculator and the second player decides to remove the 4, then 40000 must be subtracted from the number displayed to leave 12305678.

Play continues until all original digits have been removed and only zero is left in the display.

Extensions

Variations of this activity might include:

- ◆ Playing it with the whole class. The teacher calls out a number in which all the digits are different (e.g., 456.7) and has the children enter it into their calculators. Then the teacher asks the children to remove a particular digit by a subtraction operation and continues nominating digits until the display shows zero. An overhead calculator is useful when using this approach.

- ◆ Using smaller numbers (e.g., three digits) for younger children.
- ◆ Using larger and decimal numbers for older children.
- ◆ Changing the rules so that a number must be *added* rather than subtracted to change a digit. For example, in $5631 + 70 = 5701$, the three in the tens place is wiped out.
- ◆ The level of difficulty may be raised by specifying both digit and place. For example, in 5631 the teacher would specify that the 3 must be wiped out, but it must be moved to the ones column first:

$5631 \div 10 = 563.1$
$563.1 - 3 = 560.1$

Therefore, the 3 is wiped out from the ones column.

Teaching Notes

Be sure to discuss with students their methods for wiping out the digits, so that they are able to make connections to the value of the digit in each place. Often they see the digits as only a single value; that is, in the number 20 they think of the first digit as 2 rather than as two tens.

▼ MULTIPLYING BY TEN

Math Goal

Children will understand that when a number is multiplied by ten, each digit moves one column to the left (e.g., 400 becomes 4000).

Grades

3–5

Materials

Calculator for each student; paper for recording.

Activity

Children select a whole number between 1 and 100 and key this into the calculator. Next they press x 10 = and then read and record the display. Using a chart helps to highlight the patterns for discussion. (See the following chart.)

Various examples could be tried and the pattern noted for later discussion. The calculator allows children to test numbers greater than 100 to see if their pattern continues.

Start number	Multiply by 10 =	Display number
67		670
99		990

Extensions

Similar situations involving **x** 100 and **x** 1000 could be tried. Decimal starting numbers are productive in working with older children.

Teaching Notes

This activity supports understanding of the place-value system and its relationship to multiplying by ten. It avoids the trick, usually harmful to understanding in the long term, of "adding a zero." The problem with this trick becomes evident when it is applied to decimal numbers. For example:

$7 \times 10 = 70$

If a zero is added, the 7 becomes 70. The rule appears to work. However, with decimals numbers, such as 7.6 **x** 10, if a zero is added 7.6 becomes 7.60—the value remains the same. Still other children may write 70.6. The rule does not work in this case.

▼ READING NUMBERS

Math Goal

Students will be able to key in and read decimal numbers on the calculator display.

Grades

6–8

Materials

Calculator for each student; paper for recording.

Activity

Ask students to key the following numbers into the calculator, pressing +
after each. (See the chart on page 37.) The "check number" shows what the
result should be if numbers are entered correctly.

Extensions

This activity can be easily simplified for children with particular difficulties;
for example, those who mistake 14 and 41. Younger children can try whole
numbers over one hundred.

Teaching Notes

Seeing the same number expressed in different ways helps children connect
the symbol and word and visual written form. Children can be asked to explain
how they keyed in the numbers or avoided making mistakes or mis-keying.

▼ CHANGE THE NUMERAL

Math Goal

Children understand that the value of a digit changes according to the column
in which it appears.

Grades

3–5

Materials

Calculator for each child.

Activity

This activity is similar to Wipeout. Ask students to key into their calculators
the following four-digit number:

   7345

Ask them to perform one or more operations to accomplish each of the following:

   ◆ Change the number 4 into 0 so the display shows 7305.
   ◆ Change the number 3 to a 2.
   ◆ Make the number 5 into a 9

Extensions

   ◆ After each change, ask the children to explain their method; that is,

7 thousandths 5 tenths and 3 hundredths 4 tenths and 9 thousandths 14 thousandths 4 hundredths Check No. = 1.0	4 tenths and 6 hundredths 3 thousandths 8 hundredths 57 thousandths Check No. = 0.6
4 hundredths and 6 tenths 9 thousandths 27 hundredths 1 tenth 5 thousandths Check No. = 1.024	7 hundredths and 9 thousandths 2 tenths 8 hundredths and 9 thousandths 4 tenths and 6 hundredths 2 thousandths Check No. = 0.83
3 tenths and 6 hundredths 1 hundredth 7 hundredths and 8 thousandths 5 tenths and 2 thousandths 5 hundredths Check No. = 1.0	5 tenths 4 hundredths 3 tenths and 2 thousandths 1 tenth and 9 thousandths Check No. = 0.951
7 thousandths 5 hundredths 2 hundredths and 1 thousandth 1 tenth and 4 thousandths 1 tenth, 7 hundredths, 8 thousandths Check No. = 0.36	5 thousandths 5 tenths and 1 hundredth 4 thousandths 8 hundredths 1 thousandth Check No. = 0.6

what they keyed into their machine and why they selected a particular sequence. Children can be asked to select their own starting numbers and changes. This could comprise a series of student challenges designed by the class. Some changes can be made in more than one way. Children could be challenged to find alternate ways or all possible ways to make a change.

◆ Increase the level of difficulty by using decimals and larger numbers. For example: What if the number was 793.246? Children could be asked to move the 4 to the ones column, then change the 4 into a 0.

Teaching Notes

An important feature of this activity is to enable children to explain how a digit (e.g., 2) can be different from its place value (e.g., 20).

▼ LAST TO ZERO

Math Goal

Students will understand the concept of place value and be able to manipulate digits in the ones, tens, and hundreds columns.

Grades

3–5

Materials

Calculator for each student; pencil and paper for recording.

Activity

Have children work in groups of three. Each child secretly enters a three-digit number into the calculator. The players take turns guessing the digits entered by the person on their right. For example, a student has entered the number 345 onto the calculator display. Play begins when the student to his or her right (player one) asks this student (player two) if the number contains, for example, sixes. It does not, so play moves to player two, who asks a question of the student on his or her right (player three). However, if player one had asked player two if the number contained any fours, player two would have had to admit to the number and the place column involved ("I have four tens."). Player two then would have subtracted that number from his or her total, leaving 305 (the other digits remain secret). The game continues in this way until all the calculator displays read zero. Students keep track of the digits they have asked about by recording them on paper.

Extensions

◆ A competitive element can be introduced by having the first person to reach zero declared the winner.

◆ Using decimals as the initial secret number will increase the level of difficulty.

◆ A variation of this game requires players both to subtract and to add guessed numbers in place-value form. For example, if player one guesses the 3 in player two's number (345), player two subtracts 300 from the number while player one adds 300 to his or her own total. Again, the last player to reach zero wins.

◆ Another variation on this game replaces zero with a different target number.

Teaching Notes

As with any activity, it is important that children explain their strategies. When listening to children's explanations, teachers can note any misunderstandings about aspects of place value.

▼ I'LL MAKE IT ODD (OR EVEN)

Math Goal

Children will recognize odd and even numbers and the patterns associated with such numbers in equations involving the four basic operations.

Grades

6–8

Materials

Calculator for each pair of students; pencil and paper for recording.

Activity

One player writes the numbers 1 through 9 on the recording paper. The players decide between themselves who will be odd and who will be even. Player one chooses a number from the list on the recording paper, which is then keyed into the calculator. Player two performs a calculation using the number on the calculator display, one of the four basic operations (addition, subtraction, multiplication, and division), and a digit from the list of 1–9. The digit used is then crossed out and cannot be used again. The equal key is pressed and the calculator handed back to player one, who repeats this sequence using the new display number and any of the remaining digits. The players continue to take turns until all digits on the list are crossed off.

If the number left on the display is odd, then the player who selected odd is the winner. If the final display shows an even number, then the other player wins.

Rules that apply to this activity are as follows:

- Decimals are rounded at the finish.
- Division can only be used with whole numbers.

Teaching Notes

The children should describe orally or in writing their strategies for playing and winning. An example of a strategy they might use includes:

If I multiply by 2, I will always obtain an even number.

Other examples of strategies include:

odd + odd = even
odd + even = odd
even + odd = odd
odd x odd = odd
odd x even = even

▼ CUBED TO A HUNDRED

Math Goal
Children will develop their knowledge of cubic numbers.

Grades
6–8

Materials
Calculator for each student; paper and pencil for recording.

Activity
Have students key in the following equations:

$$4 \times 4 \times 4 = 64$$
$$5 \times 5 \times 5 = 125$$

Then ask them to find a number that, when multiplied by itself three times, is equal to 100. A tolerance of plus or minus 0.5 is acceptable.

Extensions

◆ Children make their own "cubed" puzzle. Teachers will need to provide the puzzle framework:

☐ x ☐ x ☐ = Answer

◆ Children select the number for the answer from within the range of 8 to 27, or 27 to 64, or 64 to 125, or 125 to 216, or another pair of consecutive cubic numbers.

Teaching Notes

Using the calculator in this situation allows the children to generate and test equations much more rapidly than would be possible using paper and pencil. Children are then able to concentrate on the problem to be solved rather than on performing tedious calculations. As always, discussion of strategies used by the children in solving the problem is important. A typical strategy might be guess-and-check.

▼ THE AVERAGE MIDDLE-SCHOOLER

Math Goal

Children will be able to identify and calculate mean, median, and mode averages.

Grades

6–8

Materials

Calculator and measuring tape for each student; paper and pencil for recording.

Activity

Set the children the task of advising a clothing manufacturer on the average measurement of a child in their grade so that the manufacturer can make appropriately sized clothes. Ask children to decide what information the manufacturer would need. The data they generate by measuring their classmates could be put into chart or table form for ease of reference. Children would produce actual measurements of arm length, leg length, height, waist circumference, and so on. They would then use the calculator to determine the mean average.

Extension
Children could be asked to write a report for the manufacturer in which they describe their data-collection techniques, results, and sizing recommendations for achieving maximum sales and minimum cost (or production waste).

Teaching Notes
The calculator allows children to work quickly and efficiently with real as opposed to contrived data. The term *average* is a global term that is often not clearly defined. It is important to clarify the mathematical meanings of *mean, median,* and *mode* and their relation to use in the world. The mean is found by adding the measurements and dividing by the total number of measurements taken. The mode is the most commonly occurring measure; more than one mode is possible.

To demonstrate the median value, the teacher could line up all the children by height. If there is an odd number of children, the median height is the midpoint. If there is an even number of children, there will be two children representing the midpoint. Their heights would need to be added and then divided by two to determine the median average.

While the calculator will assist in the calculation of the average, the real value of this activity lies in the discussion related to the appropriate use of *average* in real settings.

▼ MORE THAN ONE WAY

Math Goal
Children will understand the relationship between addition and multiplication and develop methods to solve an addition problem comprised of repeated numbers (e.g., 2 + 2 + 2) more efficiently (e.g., as 3 x 2).

Grades
3–5

Materials

Calculator for each student; pencil and paper for recording.

Activity

Ask the children to write down one way of completing the following calculations on a calculator and indicate the sequence of keystrokes they would use.

a. 6 + 6 + 6 + 6 + 6 + 6 = _____
b. 123 + 123 + 123 + 123 + 123 + 123 = _____
c. 99 + 99 + 99 + 99 + 99 + 99 + 99 = _____

Extension

Ask children to devise a simpler, more efficient, mental method for calculating the answer to problem c.

Teaching Notes

Discussion should lead to the conclusion that repeated addition of the same number is the same as multiplying that number by the number of times it appears. For example, problem b contains six groups of 123, or 6 x 123. Discussion around problem c might lead to the idea that the correct answer could be achieved mentally by replacing 99 with 100 (an easier number to work with), multiplying by 7, and then subtracting seven ones (to compensate for using 100 instead of 99), so 100 x 7 – 7. To cite a similar example, 2 x 99 = 198 is the same as 2 x 100 – 2, which can easily be done in one's head. Multiplying by 99 also produces some interesting patterns, and these could be discussed. Help children see that the outside numbers of the answer add to 9 and that the first number is one less than the multiplying number; for example, in 4 x 99 = 396, the outside numbers 3 and 6 add up to 9, and 3 is one less than the multiplying number, 4.

▼ DISAPPEARING TO ZERO

Math Goal

Children will understand the effect of dividing numbers by 10.

Grades

3–5

Materials
Four-function calculator for each student; pencil and paper for recording.

Activity
Ask the children to key a number (one or two digits) into their calculator (for example, 27), and then use the calculator to divide the number by 10 (2.7). That answer is then divided by 10 (0.27) and so on, until either an error message occurs or the number "disappears to zero." Ask them to record the stages of dividing like this:

$$27 \div 10 = 2.7$$
$$2.7 \div 10 = 0.27$$
$$0.27 \div 10 = 0.027$$

Extension
Children could be asked to explore what would happen if they divided by 100 or 1,000 instead of 10. What about if they multiplied by 10 or 100? What about if the start number is divided by 20? What happens if you start with a larger number or a decimal number? Children should see that larger numbers take longer to reach zero. However, a similar pattern emerges.

Teaching Notes
At any stage during the activity the children could be asked to say or read the number on their calculator display. Pose one or more of the following questions to have the children reflect on this activity:

How big is the number compared with the starting number?
How has the number changed?
What patterns can you see in the answers to the division problems?

▼ READING NUMBERS

Math Goal
Children are able to connect the number name with the number symbol and to develop an idea of magnitude and order.

Grades
3–5

Materials
Calculator for each student.

Activity

Ask children to press the calculator keys so that the calculator shows a large number in the display. Children must be able to read the number correctly out loud ("two, seven, three" in place of "two hundred and seventy-three" is not allowed).

Extension

Restrictions may be applied; for example, you might require the number to have a zero, but not in the ones column.

This idea could be developed into a class activity in which, for example, groups of six children are asked to form a human number line, arranging themselves in ascending order according to the numbers they have input into their calculators. Once in line, they could each be asked to state their number and justify their position. A further variation involves the teacher designating the value of the line endpoints. The children are asked to key in a number within these limits. They could be asked to not only arrange themselves in numerical order but to also position themselves proportionally along the designated line. For example, in a line with endpoints of 1 and 100, a child with a calculator number of 25 would position him- or herself approximately a quarter of the way along the line.

The "squeeze" variation requires an onlooking child to key a number into the calculator that is between two adjacent numbers on the human line—for example, between 45 and 55. This can continue until all the children are placed in the human number line. Older children could be asked to perform a calculation to produce an appropriate number on the line. Interesting situations arise when the squeeze is, for example, between 54 and 55, or the number line endpoints are 0 and 2.

Teaching Notes

The number line is an important teaching aid. It is used here to help children connect number name and number order.

▼ TELL ME ABOUT THE ANSWER

Math Goal

Children are able to judge if an answer is appropriate to the calculation undertaken, particularly when a calculator has been used.

Grades

3–5; 6–8

Materials

Calculator for each student.

Activity

Ask the class the following situation:

> Jeremy found an answer of 945 when he used his calculator to multiply 63 x 18.

Ask students to suggest why Jeremy's answer is wrong, without performing the calculation themselves. Encourage children to use their estimation skills in offering suggestions (e.g., an estimate of 60 x 20 gives 1200, which suggests that the correct answer is in the thousands place rather than the hundreds place).

Ask the children to explain, using their calculators if they wish, what Jeremy might have done to obtain the incorrect response.

Extension

Ask the children to use their mental estimation skills to explain which of the below numbers is the right answer to the equation 79 x 62 and why the others can be ruled out.

    a. 478
    b. 4671
    c. 4898
    d. 47018

Teaching Notes

Estimation is a vital element of number sense and calculator use. It should also be part of calculation using standard paper-and-pencil methods. During this activity, estimation techniques should be discussed; for example, decisions regarding order of magnitude—is the expected answer in the hundreds or thousands or larger? Intuitive checks related to odd and even numbers could be done. In the example 79 x 62, a quick calculation of 9 x 2 (the ones-place digits) gives an answer of 18; since that number is even, the answer could not possibly be odd, and we are able to rule out solution *b* in the above list.

▼ TELL ME

Math Goal

Children are able to express their knowledge and their learning goals, information that is useful to the teacher in planning appropriate instruction.

Grades

3–5; 6–8

Materials

A list (see below) for each child.

Activity

A useful discussion starter is "Tell me . . ." Ask children to complete their response to the following statements, either orally or in a written form:

> Tell me what you know about calculators.
> Tell me the best thing you can do on a calculator.
> Tell me the sort of problems you would do on a calculator.
> Tell me why you would use a calculator for those problems.
> Tell me what you would like to be able to do on a calculator
> Tell me what you do not quite understand about calculators.

Teaching Notes

You may need to ask children to clarify their responses. Often children will state that they use a calculator when numbers are large—a legitimate reason. Some statements, however, may show that children are not using appropriate mental strategies. For example, the fact that an older student offers an equation such as 70 x 40 as something to be done on the calculator suggests that the student has not yet learned the strategy of decomposing such equations; 70 x 40 decomposed into 7 x 4 x 10 x 10 can easily be solved mentally.

▼ HIT 37

Math Goal

Children will strengthen their ability to add numbers mentally.

Grades

3–5

Materials

Calculator, paper, and pencil for each pair of children.

Activity

Have each pair of children use the calculator to solve the following problem:

> Using only the numbers 1, 2, 3, 4, and 5 and the addition operation, devise a way to obtain a total of 37. Numbers can be combined as well as used repeatedly.

Extensions

Variations of this activity could include:

- allowing subtraction as well as addition to be used
- allowing any of the four basic operations to be used
- allowing each digit to be used only once
- having students start from 37 and subtract the designated numbers until they reach zero

Teaching Notes

Children will produce a variety of ways to reach 37—some may repeatedly add 1 until they reach the desired result. Others may select 35 + 2. Ask children to find more than one way to solve the problem to move them away from their obvious solutions and to engage them in thinking about numbers and addition.

▼ CLOSEST TO ONE THOUSAND

Math Goal

Children are able to practice and better understand multiplication.

Grades

3–5; 6–8

Materials

One calculator for each group of up to four; pencil and paper for recording.

Activity

Groups are asked to use the calculator to perform a calculation with the following parameters:

1. The starting number must be between 10 and 30.
2. This number must be multiplied by a number between 1 and 10.
3. The answer must then be multiplied by another number between 1 and 10.

The aim of the activity is to obtain a final result of 1000; the group that reaches 1,000 or comes closest to it without going over wins. Someone from each group records the numbers used in each attempt, as well as results (see chart below); this information is then used in subsequent attempts to reach the target number.

Starting number (10–30)	Multiply by (1–10)	Multiply by (1–10)	Answer	Comment
23	5	9	1035	Too large
23	5	8	920	Too small

Extensions

It is possible to include a scoring system whereby, for example:

The group closest to 1000 receives 5 points.
Totals over 900 score 2 points.
Totals over 1000 deduct 2 points.

Teaching Notes

The two important aspects of this activity for teachers to develop are:

◆ the role of estimation to achieve a close approximation to the required answer
◆ the understanding that multiplying by 5 and then 8 achieves the same result as multiplying by 40 (5 x 8 = 40)

▼ CLOSEST TO ONE HUNDRED

Math Goal

Children understand the effect of multiplying by one- and two-digit numbers, and are able to practice with estimation, and number relationships and patterns.

Materials

Calculator for each group of up to four children; list of "allowed" numbers (see below); pencil and paper for recording.

Activity

Working in groups, children take turns selecting a number from a list of allowed numbers provided by the teacher. Such a list might look like the following:

14	19	37	17	26
7	9	33	21	24

The first student enters one of the above numbers into the calculator and then multiplies it by a number of his or her own choice, which could be a whole number or a decimal. Student one then passes the calculator to student two, who multiplies the display number by another number of student two's own choice. Play continues for up to four children in this way until the group works out its score. The score is the difference between 100 and the "stop number"; that is, a stop number of 99.99 would receive a score of .01. After four rounds, the group with the lowest accumulated score wins. One of the students keeps track of the group's calculations using a chart like this one:

Selected number	Multiplying number	Next	Next	Next	Stop number
9	10	1.1	1.01		99.99

Extensions

List numbers as well as stop numbers can be changed. Increase the challenge by limiting the number of times that the list number can be multiplied or requiring that it be multiplied a certain number of times.

Teaching Notes

Observe children's strategies for multiplying (for example, are they using decimal numbers when they are close to the target?). Asking them to explain what they are going to do next and why helps them, as well as other children in the group, think about numbers and develop their range of strategies. It also offers the teacher information about the children's knowledge and misconceptions. For example, many children believe that multiplying a number makes it larger, although multiplying by a number less than one always makes it smaller.

▼ WITHIN 1 OF THE SUM

Math Goal
Children will strengthen their understanding of multiplying decimals.

Grades
6–8

Materials
One calculator for each pair of students; pencil and paper for recording moves (optional).

Activity
Player one sets the two- or three-digit target number. Player two sets the two-digit starting number and enters it into the calculator. The players take turns multiplying the display number by numbers of their choice, in the attempt to produce a result that is within 1 of the target number. The first person to come within 1 of the target number wins.

For example, if the starting number is 12 and the target number is 99, a record of the game might look like this:

Player 1	Target set at 99
Player 2	Start set at 12
Player 1	$12 \times 5 = 60$
Player 2	$60 \times 1.5 = 90$
Player 1	$90 \times 1.1 = 99$

Teaching Notes
This game can be used to overcome the common misconception in children that multiplying always gives a larger answer. In playing this game, students often overshoot the target number, and the next player must make the answer smaller by multiplying with a number less than one.

▼ MORE SECRET NUMBERS

Math Goal

Children find missing numbers and operations using basic algebra strategies such as complementary addition and inverse operations.

Grades

3–5

Materials

A calculator for each child; pencil and paper for recording.

Activity

Partner one enters a starting number, for example, 9, into the calculator, keeping it hidden from partner two, then records this number on paper (again keeping it hidden from partner). Partner one then performs one of the four basic operations on the number (for example, multiplication, using 12: 9 x 12) and records both the operation and the answer on a separate piece of paper. This is then presented to the second child as an equation, whose starting (or secret) number is unknown. The second child must identify the missing number and solve the equation. For the example above, the equation that would be given to the second partner would look like this:

$? \times 12 = 108$

Extension

Variations allow for the starting and finishing numbers to be declared but the operation and operation number kept secret. For example:

$6 \; ? \; ? = 48$

Teaching Notes

Children would be expected to explain their strategy for finding the missing information and solving the equation. For example, for the equation $? \times 12 = 108$, a child might suggest that ten twelves are 120, so it must be less. One lot of 12 less would be 108. The same problem could be solved by dividing 12 into 108—in other words, the inverse operation.

▼ DECIMAL CHALLENGE

Math Goal

Children see that multiplication does not always result in a larger answer. For example, multiplying by a number less than 1 will produce an answer smaller than the original (100 x 0.9 = 90). Likewise, dividing by a number less than 1 will produce an answer larger than the original (90 ÷ 0.9 = 100).

Grades
6–8

Materials
One calculator for each pair of children.

Activity
Ask the children to solve the following problem and explain their strategy.

> What could 85 be multiplied by to obtain an answer between 20 and 30?

Extension
An example of a similar problem is as follows:

> What could 85 be divided by to obtain an answer between 190 and 220?

This could be repeated using other starting numbers and answer ranges.

Teaching Notes
The idea of multiplying a number to obtain a smaller answer can be difficult for children to grasp, as it contradicts their understanding of basic multiplication. Calculators can be used to check that the idea works with various numbers, both large and small. Children could also be asked to find other numbers that could be used with 85 to obtain answers between 20 and 30.

▼ CONSTANT COUNTING

Math Goal
Children are able to see connections and relationships in multiplication by building on the idea of repeated addition.

Grades
3–5

Materials
Calculator for each student.

Activity

Children use the calculator's constant function to count by a designated amount. For example, starting with zero, to count by fives, clear the calculator and press + 5. Each time the equal key is pressed, the calculator will add five to the number shown on the display, beginning with zero. Ask the children to keep count of how many times they press the equal key. For example, if they stop at 45 they will have pressed it nine times. Nine groups of 5 total 45; this can be translated as 9 x 5 = 45.

Extension

Ask students to explore other final numbers obtained while using the constant function to count by fives. Many children will go past 10 x 5 = 50 and begin to build connections to larger numbers. Children can explore similar situations by using the constant function to count with other numbers.

Teaching Notes

A variation on this activity is called Shuteye, whereby children decide on a final number, close their eyes while pressing the equal key, and open them only when they think they have reached the designated total.

For example, the calculator may be set with a starting number of 70 by entering 70 into the display. Then, by pressing – 7, the calculator will be set to count down in sevens every time the equal key is pressed. Children could be asked to predict how many presses (10) are necessary before zero is reached. This information can then be restated as "there are 10 groups of 7 in 70," or 70 ÷ 7 = 10.

▼ EXPLORE A NUMBER

Math Goal

Students will see numbers in a variety of ways and formats, and as a result of various operations.

Grades

3–5

Materials

Calculator for each student.

Activity

The teacher selects a focus number; for example, 48. Students then explore the number by developing a series of equations that give the focus number as the result. Ask the children to obtain the focus number by using each of the operations (addition, subtraction, multiplication, division) or by using a combination of operations.

Extensions

This activity is particularly adaptable to various age groups and levels of ability. For example, younger children can be asked to use an easy focus number such as 10 and construct equations using only addition, subtraction, and multiplication. Older or more able children can be offered challenges that involve, for example, fractions, prime numbers, or square numbers.

Teaching Notes

This activity is useful when used with children as a routine exercise. It provides plenty of opportunity for discussion, touches on several aspects of number sense, may be employed as a reference point for assessment purposes, and can be used to show the limitations of calculators that do not use order-of-operations logic.

▼ PREDICTING THE DIGITS

Math Goal

Children develop their estimation strategies and ability to make sense of calculations.

Grades

6–8

Materials

Calculator for each pair of children.

Activity

Pose the following question to the class:

> When a two-digit number is multiplied by a three-digit number, how many digits would you expect to find in the answer?

Have them discuss the question and make a prediction, then use the calculator to test their conjectures. The discussion should lead children to conclude that a two-digit number, multiplied by a three-digit number, will produce a four- or five-digit result.

Extension

Encourage children to generate similar questions, such as "How many digits would I expect the answer to contain if a three-digit number is multiplied by a three-digit number?" or "How many digits would I expect to find in the answer if I multiplied a five-digit number by a four-digit number?" The latter question could lead to a discussion of calculator limitations, since the display of a simple four-function calculator allows a maximum of only eight digits to be displayed.

Teaching Notes

Use of the calculator in this activity enables children to focus more fully on investigating the question, since the exploratory calculations—which would be tedious to perform with paper and pencil—are done quickly and accurately. A key goal of this activity is for children to understand patterns in multiplication that may later be used as an intuitive check for an answer to a calculation. For example, a two-digit number, multiplied by a two-digit number, will produce a three- or four-digit answer; a three-digit-by-three-digit multiplication will produce a five- or six-digit answer.

▼ GET THE POINT

Math Goal

Children develop an understanding of the effect of operations on decimal numbers—in particular, on the position of the decimal point.

Grades

6–8

Materials

Calculator for each student; pencil and paper for recording.

Activity

Present the following situation to the class:

> When calculating the results of the following problems, Kit forgot to include the decimal point. Without recalculating the result, place the decimal point where you believe it belongs.

376.74 + 239.2 = 61594
7.51 − 0.04 = 747
32.56 x 2.1 = 68376

Ask the children to explain how they decided where to place the decimal point. Tell them to test their theory by using the calculator to check other calculations. They must predict the outcome before they do the calculation.

Extensions

Vary the operation so that children are able to make conjectures related to each operation. The size of numbers and the number of decimal places could be increased to test other patterns.

Teaching Notes

Often children are taught a rule for working out where to place the decimal point. Such rules involve setting up the equation so that the decimal points are aligned or counting the places to the right of the decimal point and applying this to the answer. For example, 7.5 x 6.25 is completed in the same way as 75 x 625. The answer, 46875, is found and then the decimal point is placed by counting the number of digits to the right of the decimal point in the *original calculation* (in other words, three digits). Next, the decimal point in the answer is placed by counting three places to the left from the far right digit (5), in other words, 46.875.

Children using these rules may have little understanding of decimals. If children have been exposed to activities emphasizing patterns and have been able to reflect on such activities and develop their number sense, there is no need for short-term, noncontextual rules to determine where to place the decimal point.

▼ HIT THE RANGE

Math Goal

Children understand the effect of multiplying by whole numbers and decimals and are able to make appropriate estimates.

Grades

6–8

Materials

Calculator for each pair of students; pencil and paper for recording.

Activity

One child chooses a range of numbers (e.g., 630 to 660), while the other chooses a starting number (e.g., 47).

The first student enters the starting number into the calculator and presses the multiplication key followed by an estimate designed to place the result within the chosen range. For example, she might press 47 x 15. Pressing the equal key would produce an answer of 705.

This answer does not lie within the chosen range and therefore the calculator is passed to the second student. The second student must then use the 705 in the display as a starting point and multiply 705 by a number so that the answer lies between 630 and 660. Multiplying by 0.9, for example, would produce a desired result of 634.5.

Extensions

The range could be designated by the teacher to highlight aspects of classroom work; for example, if instruction is on decimals, the teacher could pick a range that lies between two decimal numbers.

Teaching Notes

The expression "operation sense" refers to an understanding of the effect of multiplying by powers of ten, an understanding of estimation, and the relative magnitude of numbers. This activity helps develop children's operation sense.

▼ SHOW ME THIS ON A CALCULATOR

Math Goal

Children understand the limitations of an eight-digit-display calculator.

Grades

6–8

Materials

Four-function calculator for each student; pencil and paper for recording and calculating.

Activity

Ask children to attempt the following calculation on a calculator:

100000027 x 6952

Since four-function calculator displays cannot accommodate the answer to this problem, children are asked to devise another way to obtain the answer.

Teaching Notes

To solve this question children need to draw on place-value knowledge and make use of some interim records. Children can simplify the above calculation to 100000000 x 6952, which is relatively easy to do mentally if one has an understanding of place value. On the other hand, 27 x 6952 is more problematic and would be much more efficiently completed with the aid of a calculator. The results of these two interim calculations could then be combined using pencil and paper to produce a result.

▼ THIS CAN BE DIVIDED BY . . .

Math Goal

Children will begin to develop an understanding of factors and multiples and relationships in numbers that inform decisions about divisibility.

Grades

3–5; 6–8

Materials

Calculator for each student.

Activity

Show the children that whole numbers ending in zero in the ones column are exactly divisible by ten. Have them check this fact by using a calculator; make sure they verify that very large numbers ending in zero are also exactly divisible by ten.

Children are then challenged to explore other divisibility rules; for example, which whole numbers are exactly divisible by 5 or 2. They will need to use the calculator to generate and test data to formulate and check their theories.

Extensions

Division rules that are especially useful to check are those that apply to multiples of certain numbers, for example, 3, 6, 9 and 2, 4, 8; similarities between such rules can be highlighted.

Teaching Notes

Once children have a little background and understanding, it might be useful to introduce well-known rules; for example, if the digits of a number add up to nine, then the number is divisible by nine.

▼ WHAT'S HAPPENING HERE?

Math Goal

Children will reflect on the idea that when a number less than one is multiplied by a whole number, the answer will be smaller than the starting number. This fact is in conflict with the beliefs of many children, who think that multiplying a number always makes it larger.

Grades

6–8

Materials

Calculator for each pair of students; pencil and paper for recording.

Activity

Ask each pair of students to generate a list of numbers; for example:

    65   72   187   23   5   689   1234

One of the students then multiplies each of the numbers by a number slightly less than 1 (for example, 0.9), while the other student multiplies the same numbers by a number slightly more than 1 (for example, 1.1). These multipliers will produce answers slightly smaller and slightly larger than the original numbers. Both partners keep a written record of the number, the multiplier, and the answer, using a chart like the one shown on page 61.

Partners compare their answers and comment on the relationships that are revealed.

Extension

Students can check other multipliers that are close together and near to 1 to confirm their ideas.

Teaching Notes

This exercise can be effectively partnered with the activities Closest to One Hundred and Within One of the Sum.

Number	Multiplier	Answer	Comment
65			
72			
187			
23			
5			
689			
1234			

▼ BROKEN KEYS

Math Goal
Children will be engaged in thinking about numbers, spotting relationships in them, and breaking numbers into parts.

Grades
3–5; 6–8

Materials
Calculator for each child; pencil and paper for recording.

Activity
Present the children with a calculation, for example:

278 + 708 =

Ask them to work out the answer on the calculator, but *without* pressing the 7 key or the 8 key. You could place a colored sticker over the keys to remind the children that these keys are "broken" and not available for this activity.

Ask them to record their keystrokes. This serves as a way to check that they have not used the 7 and 8 keys in calculating the result.

Extension

When children have found one way to solve the equation and have recorded and explained it, challenge them to find a different way to solve the problem. You can easily vary this activity by prohibiting the use of other number keys or including operation keys among those that are "broken," making numbers to be calculated larger or smaller, or requiring that a particular operation be used in the solution.

Teaching Notes

This activity forces children to consider the size and value of numbers within a calculation, something that they do not often do when using standard methods of calculation.

▼ CALCULATOR BATTLESHIPS

Math Goal

Children strengthen their estimating skills through practice.

Grades

6–8

Materials

Calculator for each pair of students.

Activity

Students must first be supplied with a completed weapons list and a fleet sheet for each player. These can be devised initially by the teacher and later by other students. The weapons sheet is a list of calculations; the fleet sheets contain the answers to these calculations, arbitrarily arranged. During play, the answers become the "targets"; a student scores a "hit" against the opposing fleet by matching an equation or, "weapon," with its appropriate response. Example weapons list and fleet sheets are given below.

Weapons List

25 x 65	567 – 349
273 + 426	412 ÷ 4
1234 – 942	49 x 21
9 x 72	369 ÷ 3
550 x 2000	695 + 310
333 + 987	102 x 99

Fleet Sheets

FLEET ONE

1029	218
699	1005
1320	123

FLEET TWO

648	10098
1625	1100000
292	103

The children select a fleet and then take turns firing. A shot is undertaken in the following way: The "admiral" of fleet one identifies a target number in fleet two and declares it. The admiral then selects a weapon from the list, declares this to his opponent, and keys the equation into the calculator. If the weapon produces an answer that is the same as the declared target, that "ship" is sunk (crossed out on the opponent's fleet sheet). A wrong answer, even if it is in the attached fleet, is counted as a miss. The game continues until one fleet is sunk.

Extension

Children can be challenged to design a similar game either for younger children or for their peers. Teachers may wish to stipulate the size of numbers and which operations are to be used, especially if the game is designed for younger children.

Teaching Notes

Each player or "admiral" should be able to explain their tactics and strategies for firing. Teachers can suggest that guessing is not a useful game plan. They might add a section that requires the admirals to state the reason for their selection of target and weapons.

▼ BLANKS

Math Goal

Children pay attention to the value and properties of numbers rather than seeing them as digits to be manipulated.

Materials

For each student, a page of problems containing blanks (or triangles; see below), and a calculator for testing ideas.

Activity

Show the children an equation with parts of the calculation blanked out or replaced with triangles. The children are then asked to discover the missing digits. Here are two examples:

a. $\triangle$ 8   b. $\triangle \triangle - \triangle$ 8 = 24
   + 3 $\triangle$
   ‾‾‾‾
    67

Ask children to explain why their set of digits works in each of the calculations.

Extension
A similar activity involves using mock-ups of old homework books in which ink has been spilled on some of the numbers. Children pretend to be museum curators with the job of restoring the original manuscript.

Teaching Notes
The numbers that are concealed or the operations used can be varied to suit the needs of the children (e.g., multiplication can be used with older children).

▼ THE SPLITS

Math Goal
Children will develop flexible methods of calculation by exploring the distributive property of numbers.

Grades
3–5

Materials
Calculator for each student; pencil and paper for recording.

Activity
Ask the children to complete and note the following:

   7 x 8 = $\triangle$

Then ask them to split the 7 into 4 and 3. Next, they have to multiply 4 x 8 and 3 x 8 and add both answers together. Finally, they have to talk about what they notice. From here, they can explore the distributive property of multiplication with other combinations of two numbers that add up to 7. Other multiplications can be used (for example, 9 x) to see if their idea always works.

Extensions

Children could try to explain the relationship between the original calculation and the new calculation that utilizes "split numbers." They could discuss how it relates to the standard method for multiplying numbers. They could also try larger numbers, such as 36 **x** 42. Have children explore the following questions:

What happens if one of the numbers is broken into three parts?

What happens if the other number is split; for instance, in the above example, if the 8 is split instead of the 7?

What happens if the question is split using multiplication rather than addition? For example, 7 **x** 8 becomes 7 **x** 4 **x** 2. Here the 8 is split with multiplication into 4 **x** 2.

Teaching Notes

Reflection, discussion, and testing of theories and observations with the calculator as a number generator are important. Children might then report their findings and observations in writing. Connections to standard algorithms will help children see and possibly understand what is happening within the algorithm and allow them to make sense of the procedure, as well as be flexible in its application.

▼ TRY, TRY, AND TRY AGAIN

Math Goal

Children are able to make decisions about and observe the effects of one number on another and the magnitude of answers.

Grades

6–8

Materials

Calculator for each pair of children; pencil and paper for recording.

Activity

Set for the students the following task:

Using only the 1, 2, 3, and 4 keys and the **x** operation, make equations that produce the largest and the smallest possible totals.

Extension

Similar tasks can be developed that use a different operation or different numbers. Ask students to write about what they have done and any patterns or relationships that they have noticed.

Teaching Notes

Students who complete this task will be more engaged than children who are asked to simply complete a set of textbook problems, because it involves looking for patterns and forming and testing conjectures, activities that help develop children's number sense. The next activity, The Largest Product, is similar but shows how creating a template can change the task while retaining the underlying idea.

▼ THE LARGEST PRODUCT

Math Goal

Children understand the effect of the digits when they are placed in different columns in a standard calculation layout.

Grades

6–8

Materials

Calculator for each student; pencil and paper for recording.

Activity

Ask the children to choose three different digits, for example 9, 5, and 4. Then have them try different combinations of these digits to produce the largest answer in the given format. For example:

$$\Delta \times \Delta \times \Delta$$

or

$$\Delta\Delta \times \Delta$$

or

$$\Delta \times \Delta\Delta$$

Children could also be asked to order their answers from smallest to largest.

Extension
Ask them to try starting with four or five digits.

Teaching Notes
Reflection should emphasize how digits can be placed to produce the largest answer. Children could also be required to explain the strategy for the digit placement.

▼ ODD AND EVEN

Math Goal
Children will understand the properties of odd and even numbers.

Grades
3–5

Materials
Calculator for each child.

Activity
Ask children to try the following types of calculations on a calculator and be prepared to report their answers to the rest of the class.

> odd number + odd number = ?
> even number + even number = ?
> odd number + even number = ?

Extensions
Further developments could ask children to try the same activity with more than two numbers, for example, ODD, ODD, EVEN, to identify other relationships.

If five numbers are added together, ask children how many of them must be odd so that the product is odd.

Changing the function from addition to subtraction or multiplication develops the investigation further, as in the following:

> odd number x odd number = ?
> even number x even number = ?
> odd number x even number = ?

Teaching Notes

Children will need to describe what they have noticed and offer some general statements about relationships between odd numbers and even numbers.

▼ MAKING MISTAKES

Math Goal

Children further their understanding of estimating the answer to a calculation performed on a calculator or checking the sense of calculations performed by standard methods.

Grades

3–5

Materials

Calculator for each student.

Activity

Present students with a situation such as the following:

> Elizabeth meant to press the following keys on the calculator: 6 x 2. However, she accidentally pressed one wrong key. The calculator display showed 8 as the answer. Which keys might she have pressed?

Children can be offered other problems to solve once they have discussed their answer. For example:

15 + 5	Display shows 3
8 + 6	Display shows 48

Extension

Mistakes can involve both numbers and operations or both.

Teaching Notes

This activity again engages children in thinking about the values of numbers. Marking someone's work, pretending to be the teacher, or commenting on what other people have completed are useful activities. An important technique for children to develop when using calculators is to estimate the answer first by mental methods so that they can judge the appropriateness of the final outcome.

▼ FIND A DIFFERENT WAY

Math Goal

Children are able to make sense of calculations and select the most appropriate strategy to solve problems.

Grades

3–5

Materials

Calculator for each child or for each pair of children.

Activity

Give pairs of children or individuals the following task:

> Use your calculator to find four different ways to work out the answer to 27 + 96.

Extension

Children must describe both orally and in written form their different ways to do the calculation, for example 27 + 90 + 6.

Teaching Notes

This activity offers evidence of the way in which calculators support children's exploration of numbers. For example, children may choose to develop a way to solve 27 + 96 mentally. Exploring with a calculator may lead to a mental method; in other words, children may note a simpler way to solve this and similar problems without the use of a calculator. For example, the equation 23 + 100 will produce the same result and can be done efficiently in the student's head.

▼ MORE THAN ONE WAY TO CALCULATE

Math Goal

Children gain practice in exploring numbers and mathematical situations.

Grades

6–8

Materials

Calculator for each pair of children; pencil and paper for recording.

Activity

Give the class the following task:

> Show four different ways to calculate 300 x 400. Use a calculator to verify your methods.

Extension

Ask children to write down and explain their methods and to describe any patterns they notice.

Teaching Notes

The above activity may look out of place in a book about calculator use, particularly since it involves numbers that may easily be calculated mentally. This particular example has been included because it was given to the authors by an eleven-year-old as an example of a problem that she would complete on a calculator. The reason given for using a calculator was that the question involved big numbers. This is, at first sight, quite true; the numbers are large and a child would usually expect to do three-digit by three-digit multiplication by a standard paper-and-pencil method or using a calculator. The use of calculators to solve a question like the one above should not be encouraged, however, because with a little insight and discussion with the teacher it can easily be completed mentally by most older elementary school children. The calculator could be used to help generate alternative ways to calculate 300 x 400 and to illuminate for the child the patterns and relationships it contains. Several possibilities are:

> 3 x 4 x 100 x 100
> 300 x 4 x 100
> (100 x 400) + (100 x 400) + (100 x 400)
> (300 x 200) + (300 x 200)

Children who are reluctant to try out various combinations for fear of producing an incorrect answer are free to experiment on their calculator, where the answer is displayed only to them. Children who would quite easily lose interest in such calculations if forced to do them by hand are able to think about the question and the patterns that are revealed, since the calculations are done quickly and accurately with a calculator. If children are allowed *easy* access (not necessarily *free* access) to calculators, they will be allowed to choose when the calculator will be of benefit to them. Eventually, children, with the benefit of appropriate teacher input, will come to an understanding of the distributive property with respect to multiplication and addition (e.g., that 300 x 400 may be broken into smaller chunks that are added). Thus, 300 x 400 is the same as (150 x 400) + (150 x 400). The distributive property is the basis upon which the standard written algorithm for multiplication works. The use of the calculator, exploration, and discussion allows children to develop mathematical understandings and to progress beyond the limitations of the written procedure. Obviously, it should not be assumed that children will gain an understanding of this property as a result of a single activity. Children need to be given many opportunities with the same kind of activity to encourage thinking. The same activity could be revisited with a slight change of numbers in the activity Show Me How.

▼ SHOW ME HOW

Math Goal

Children are able to develop flexible methods of mental computation and to calculate mentally with large numbers.

Grades

6–8

Materials

Calculator for each student; paper and pencil for recording.

Activity

Give the children the following challenge:

> Show four different ways to calculate 320 x 170.
> Now see if you can find even more ways.
> Record your responses and take note of any patterns you notice.

Here are two examples of how this equation might be calculated:

> (320 x 100) + (320 x 50) + (320 x 20)
> (300 x 100) + (20 x 100) + (300 x 70) + (20 x 70)

Teaching Notes

The value of a routine activity such as this should not be underestimated. Repeating activities gives children the opportunity to play with numbers, to break them down, and to make conjectures. Children should be asked to discuss their findings in order to reinforce their learning and expose them to the ideas of their classmates. The various approaches they learn about will eventually form part of their calculating "toolbox."

▼ DESCRIBE WHAT IS HAPPENING

Math Goal

Children are able to identify patterns and relationships, enabling them to generate answers to calculations.

Grades

6–8

Materials

Calculator and Equation Patterns Table (see below) for each child.

Activity

Give students the following instructions:

1. Use your calculator to work out the first three answers in each column of the Equation Patterns Table.
2. Predict the answers for the rest of the equations in each column.
3. Check your predictions using your calculator. Correct them as necessary.
4. Describe, in writing, the patterns you discovered.

Equation Patterns Table

37 x 3 = ____	99 x 13 = ____	143 x 7 = ____
37 x 6 = ____	99 x 24 = ____	143 x 14 = ____
37 x 9 = ____	99 x 35 = ____	143 x 21 = ____
37 x 12 = ____	99 x 46 = ____	143 x 28 = ____
37 x 15 = ____	99 x 57 = ____	143 x 35 = ____
37 x 18 = ____	99 x 68 = ____	143 x 42 = ____
37 x 21 = ____	99 x 79 = ____	143 x 49 = ____

Extension

This activity can be followed with Predict and Extend, which is much less structured and relies on the calculator to generate data rapidly, so that patterns may be observed, predicted, and verified.

Teaching Notes

Children will probably notice a pattern beginning to form after completing the first three calculations. They should be encouraged to predict and verify the result for the fourth calculation and then use the pattern they have found to establish the answers to the rest of the equations. The numbers in the Equation Patterns Table have been selected because they produce obvious patterns; note that 3 x 37 = 111 and 99 x anything is the same as multiplying by 100 and subtracting one lot of the number.

▼ PREDICT AND EXTEND

Math Goal
Children will manipulate equations in a certain way to strengthen their concept of relationships and patterns.

Grades
6–8

Materials
Calculator for each child; pencil and paper for recording.

Activity
Demonstrate to the children that 20 x 20 = 400. Ask them to predict what the result would be if 1 were subtracted from the first number and added to the second, leaving 19 x 21. Have them verify their prediction using a calculator and comment on the answer, their prediction, and how the answer differs from the answer to 20 x 20. Next, have them partner with another student and check other pairs of numbers using the "subtract 1, add 1" approach, to see if they are able to observe a pattern that holds true. Have them look at smaller numbers (6 x 6) as well as larger numbers (546 x 546). Ask them to try to describe the pattern in general terms.

Extension
Challenge children by asking, "What happens if you subtract 2 and add 2 to the starting numbers?" (e.g., 3 x 3 = 9 becomes 1 x 5 = 5). Have them try out this approach with other numbers to see if they can determine a pattern that holds true.

Teaching Notes
A child with access to a calculator is far more likely to persevere with investigations like the one above than is a child who is expected to do the calculations

with pencil and paper. Children experiencing difficulties with computation may not be able to participate in the task at all without making use of a calculator. Children with poor number skills working without a calculator could easily make mistakes, and their ability to observe a pattern in this activity would be undermined.

▼ FINDING PI?

Math Goal
Children are able to find the approximate value of pi.

Grade
6–8

Materials
Calculator for each child, a collection of circular and cylindrical objects, measuring tapes, and a recording sheet (see example below).

Activity
Ask students to collect circumference and diameter measurements from a range of objects, record them on a sheet as shown below, and then divide the circumference by the diameter to find the value for pi.

Extensions
Children can investigate the origins of pi and look at its uses in other situations.

Object	Circumference	Diameter	Circumference ÷ Diameter
CD			
Plate			
Roll of tape			
Can			

Teaching Notes

The calculator may be used to perform the tedious division calculations, thereby freeing children to concentrate on looking for patterns in the numbers. By finding the approximate value of pi the children are more able to connect its meaning to context.

▼ LARGE NUMBERS

Math Goal

Children are able to think about large numbers and evaluate the answer to a calculation.

Grades

6–8

Materials

Calculator for each student.

Activity

Give the following task to the class:

> If 7326 x 634 = 4644684, what are the answers to the following calculations? Use the information in this calculation to help you predict the answers:
>
> 732.6 x 634
> 732.6 x 6.34
> 0.7326 x 6340
> 7.326 x 63.4
>
> Be ready to explain how these multiplication equations are similar to but also different from one another. Explain how you know what the answer will be without doing the calculation. Use the calculator to verify your prediction.

Extension

Have children test their predictions with other combinations of numbers. Ask them to use the calculator as a support to devise other questions similar to the example.

Teaching Notes

Before the availability of calculators, math-learning activities had to be contrived to prevent children from encountering large numbers and calculations that they would not be able to solve with pencil and paper. In many cases, this meant avoiding complex, realistic number situations.

▼ PUT THESE IN ORDER

Math Goal

Children are able to order fractions according to their size.

Grades

6–8

Materials

Calculator for each child.

Activity

Offer the children a series of fractions and ask them to put them in order of size from the smallest to the largest.

$$\frac{1}{2}, \frac{2}{3}, \frac{3}{7}, \frac{4}{5}$$

They may make a prediction of the order, which is then tested by completing the calculation on a calculator (e.g., 1 ÷ 2 = 0.5) and considering the numbers in decimal form.

Extension

Children could design their own sequences of fractions to compare.

Teaching Notes

Children have a tendency to calculate the relative size of fractions by drawing a pie diagram and dividing it into pieces equal in number to the denominator (the number under the line). At a simple level this is effective, as $\frac{1}{2}$ can be compared with $\frac{1}{4}$ and the difference in size easily seen. This is not, however, a useful strategy when one has to compare more complex fractions, such as $\frac{3}{7}$ and $\frac{5}{9}$.

Converting to decimals offers another strategy. For many children, $\frac{1}{2}$ is a useful benchmark against which to compare other fractions in an initial sorting. Two groups are formed—one that is larger than $\frac{1}{2}$ and one that is smaller. Finer grading is then completed.

A misconception held by many children is that the larger the number of the denominator, the larger the fraction. The opposite is true, but their understanding of whole numbers strongly influences their thinking with respect to fractions. When used as a teaching and learning aid, the calculator can serve to challenge this idea and help children develop a sounder understanding of fractions.

▼ SQUEEZE (2)

Math Goal
Children are able to practice conceptualizing and ordering fractions.

Grades
3–5

Materials
Calculator for each child; number-line playing board (see below); colored marker pens.

Activity
Have the children work in pairs. Each player chooses two numbers from a list designated by the teacher (e.g., 1, 2, 3, 4, 5, 6, 7, 8, 9, 10, 11, 12) to produce a fraction by placing the smaller digit as the numerator (e.g., 7 and 8 to make $\frac{7}{8}$). The fraction is then placed in the appropriate place on a number line like the one shown below. Players use different-colored markers to differentiate their markings. The idea behind the game is for one player to put three marks (representing their fractions) in a row without the other player "squeezing" a fraction in between. Players may use numbers more than once. Calculators are used to convert fractions to decimals so that they can be compared.

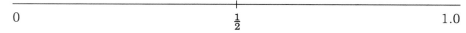

| 0 | $\frac{1}{2}$ | 1.0 |

Extensions
Allow the children to devise their own lists of possible numbers as well as to determine the endpoints of the number line.

Teaching Notes
After a few games, it is useful to have the children discuss their strategies for

selecting the fractions and for squeezing between the marks placed by their opponent. It is helpful to play Squeeze (2) as a follow-up activity to Put These in Order.

▼ BEST-BUY SURVEY

Math Goal
Children gain experience making decisions in real-world contexts with complex data.

Grades
3–5; 6–8

Materials
Calculator and examples of supermarket flyers and newspaper advertisements for each student.

Activity
Ask the children to select a particular supermarket item—for example, detergent, toothpaste, or dog food—and generate a data list by collecting information on various brand names, product sizes, and weight and cost of items found in the flyers and ads. These data are then used to determine which product offers the best buy or value, and the calculator is used to perform calculations that cannot easily be performed in the head.

Teaching Notes
The supermarket provides an excellent context for real-world mathematics. Parents and children alike are faced with making decisions as they shop, and these decisions frequently involve numbers. There are a variety of different brands of the same product, which come in different sizes and cost different amounts. Such situations can require one to pose and solve mathematical questions. For example, is it better to buy Brand A at x or Brand B at y? Is the extra large size of Brand C a better value than the medium size of Brand C?

▼ SPEND A MILLION DOLLARS

Math Goal
Children gain experience producing a budget or balance sheet and reading, writing, and saying large numbers.

Grades
3–5

Materials
Calculator for each child; consumer-oriented information such as mail-order catalogs, newspaper advertisements, and real estate and vacation brochures.

Activity
A favorite activity for many children (and adults) is to pretend to have won a million dollars in the lottery. Tell the children to imagine that they have each won a million dollars and have to spend it all. They must, however, keep a record to account for what has happened to the money. Children may then search through newspapers and catalogs for items to buy, using the list prices of items to create a balance sheet. The calculator can be used as necessary as they do their budget calculations.

Teaching Notes
This activity provides a useful opportunity to have children read, write, and say large numbers. Rounding and estimating with large numbers can also be attempted.

▼ HOW OLD ARE YOU?

Math Goal
Children gain experience using large numbers in problems.

Grades
3–5

Materials
Calculator for each child.

Activity
Give children the problem of using the calculator to work out how old they are in minutes (or weeks or days or seconds).

Extension
Have them solve a related problem:

Have you been alive for a million seconds?

≤

Teaching Notes

Such a problem may require children to figure out how to use the calculator to deal with numbers that their calculator display may not accommodate. This activity is often useful to present to parents at a parent evening, since it illustrates that while a calculator might help with various parts of the calculation, the student must be actively engaged in deciding how to solve the problem—what strategies to use and keys to press and in which order. In particular, knowledge of conversion factors from days to hours, minutes, and seconds is required to complete this problem.

▼ FOUR STEPS TO ZERO

Math Goal

Children gain experience using the four operations in problems.

Grades

6–8

Materials

Calculator for each student.

Activity

Ask the children to select a four-digit number and enter it into their calculators (for example, 6,724). They now have to reduce this number to zero in exactly four steps. They can use any of the four operations (+, −, x, ÷) and any two-digit numbers. Offer them an example such as the following:

Step 1	6724 − 24 = 6700
Step 2	6700 ÷ 67 = 100
Step 3	100 ÷ 10 = 10
Step 4	10 − 10 = 0

Have children report to the class any strategies they found to be effective in doing this exercise.

Extension

Use three-digit or five-digit numbers to start. Vary the number of required steps.

Teaching Notes

This is quite a difficult task and you may want children to work in pairs to minimize initial frustrations. The sharing of strategies and insights by the whole class is important. The task can be made easier by allowing children to start with three-digit numbers and use unlimited steps.

▼ STEPPING DOWN TO ONE

Math Goal
Children gain experience using the four operations in problems.

Grades
6–8

Materials
Calculator for each student.

Activity
First, ask children to select a starting number less than 100 (e.g., 46). Second, ask them to select a single-digit number from 0 to 9 (e.g., 4). Then, using only the four basic operation keys and their single-digit number (which they can use to make double-digit numbers), ask them to reduce the starting number to 1 in as few steps as possible. Offer an example such as the following (here we are using the start number 46 and the single-digit 4):

Step 1	46 + 44 = 90
Step 2	90 x 4 = 360
Step 3	360 + 44 = 404
Step 4	404 + 44 = 448
Step 5	448 – 4 = 444
Step 5	444 ÷ 444 = 1

Extensions
Groups of children might attempt to do this activity using all the numbers in a decade (e.g., all the 40s). Others could try the same number in different ways either with the same single digit or with a different one.

Teaching Notes
Children could share their thoughts on useful strategies to aid others in their search for fewer steps. The activity provides opportunities for lots of focused practice with and thinking about numbers.

.GETS

Math Goal
Children gain practice using the four basic operations in problems.

Grades
3–5; 6–8

Materials
Calculator for each child; pencil and paper for recording.

Activity
Ask children to select a target number (e.g., 12), and a single-digit operating number (e.g., 4). Challenge them to obtain the target number (the answer) in as many different ways as they can using the operating number and any of the four basic function keys. Their records of possible ways to reach the target are kept for reflection and discussion. An example of a record using the target number 12 and operating number 4 is as follows:

12 can be made as

$$4 + 4 + 4$$
$$4 + 4 + 4 + 4 - 4$$
$$44 + 4 \div 4$$

Extensions
Target numbers and operating numbers can be varied. The class can be challenged to use special target numbers (for example, the date) as part of a classroom routine.

Teaching Notes
The idea of a target can be used in various formats and with many different limitations or rules. The use of limitations and rules is a good way to challenge children with higher ability.

▼ HOW NEAR TO THE TARGET?

Math Goal
Children gain practice using the four basic operations in problems.

Grades

3–5; 6–8

Materials

Calculator for each student; pencil and paper for recording; examples below written on the board.

Activity

Ask children to place the designated digits in the boxes so that they combine to reach an answer as close to the target as possible.

☐☐ ÷ ☐
Target 10
Use 7, 8, 9

☐☐ ÷ ☐
Target 3
Use 2, 6, 9

☐☐ ÷ ☐☐
Target 4
Use 1, 2, 5, 8

☐☐ x ☐
Target 80
Use 2, 3, 5

☐☐ x ☐☐
Target 800
Use 1, 2, 3, 6

☐☐☐ ÷ ☐☐
Target 5
Use 1, 3, 4, 6, 8

Extensions

Children can investigate all possible targets for each situation shown above. Have them comment on any patterns, relationships, or strategies noticed.

Teaching Notes

As part of the reflection and reporting time, children could be asked to describe their strategies for digit placement. A variation on the target activity is to designate the function, the target, and the structure of the calculation. Children are then required to think of ways to find a near answer (target). Estimations, employment of number facts, and lots of mental calculation are generally involved before the problem is solved. The calculator is merely a support for calculations as necessary. This is another example of a calculator-available task that requires children to think about numbers in flexible ways.

▼ WHAT'S STILL MUDDY?

Math Goal

Children express what they know or do not know about calculators or specific mathematics content.

Grades

3–5; 6–8

Materials

A "muddy sheet" (see below) for each child.

Activity

Ask children to complete this sheet at the end of an activity or series of activities. You could use their responses to establish a private dialogue with individual children.

> *The Muddy Sheet*
>
> Please answer the questions below so that I can help you with your mathematics learning:
>
> What have you learned by doing this calculator activity (or activities)?
>
> What are you still unsure (or "muddy") about?
>
> What do you want to learn next about this subject?

Teaching Notes

Their answers to these questions provide one way to assess children's knowledge of the content of your teaching. They could provide valuable information for planning and further mathematics instruction.

▼ WHAT NUMBER IS THIS?

Math Goal

Children will provide the teacher with information about their knowledge of the four basic operations and of number relationships.

Grades

3–5

Materials

Calculator for each student; pencil and paper for recording.

Activity

Ask the children to figure out what number is being looked for, by solving a series of equations or by answering a set of questions. They will need to record how they have identified the secret number as well as explain any patterns and relationships they notice and use. Below are some examples.

What number is this?

4 + 5 + 6   4 x 4 – 1   (100 – 40) ÷ 4

What number is this?
It is a square number.
If you subtract 4 you can divide it exactly by 6
Its digits add up to 10

Extension
The sets of questions can form part of a bulletin board or display to be used by other children.

Teaching Notes
Assessable aspects of these tasks include the number operations children select to use, use of order of operations, relationships noted, data-gathering methods, and knowledge of special numbers such as square or prime numbers.

REFERENCES

Australian Association of Mathematics Teachers. 1986. *A National Statement on the Use of Calculators for Mathematics in Australian Schools.* Canberra: Curriculum Development Centre.

Cockcroft, W. 1982. *Mathematics Counts.* London: HMSO.

Dick, T. 1988. "The Continuing Calculator Controversy." *Arithmetic Teacher* 35 (8): 37–41.

Duffin, J. 1994. "Calculators: Do They Inhibit or Enhance Mathematical Thinking?" *Micromath* 10 (3): 25–28.

Groves, S., and K. Stacey. 1998. "Calculators in Primary Mathematics: Exploring Numbers Before Teaching Algorithms." In *The Teaching and Learning of Algorithms in School Mathematics*, edited by L. Morrow and M. Kenny. Pages 120–129. Reston, VA: National Council of Teachers of Mathematics.

Hembree, R., and D. Dessart. 1986. "Effects of Hand-Held Calculators in Pre-College Mathematics Education: A Meta-Analysis." *Journal for Research in Mathematics Education* 17 (2): 83–89.

———. 1992. "Research on Calculators in Mathematics Education." In *Calculators in Mathematics Education*, edited by J. Fey and C. Hirsch. Pages 23–32. Reston, VA: National Council of Teachers of Mathematics.

Johnson, D. C. 1985. "Calculators: Abuses and Uses." In *Calculators in the Primary School: Readings from Mathematics in Schools and Mathematics Teaching*. Pages 31–34. Leicester: Association of Teachers of Mathematics/The Mathematical Association.

Koop, A. J. 1979. "Calculators in Schools: Some Curriculum Considerations." *Australian Mathematics Teacher* 35 (4): 6–7.

McIntosh, A., B. J. Reys, and R. E. Reys. 1997. "Mental Computation in the Middle Grades: The Importance of Thinking Strategies." *Mathematics Teaching in the Middle School* 2 (5): 322–327.

National Council of Teachers of Mathematics. 1980. *Agenda for Action: Recommendations for School Mathematics*. Reston, VA: National Council of Teachers of Mathematics.

———. 2000. *Principles and Standards for School Mathematics*. Reston, VA: National Council of Teachers of Mathematics.

Reys, B. J., and R. E. Reys. 1987. "Calculators in the Classroom: How Can We Make It Happen?" *Arithmetic Teacher* 34 (6): 12–14.